Construction Accounting

A Practitioner's Guide

Steven M. Bragg

Published by AccountingTools, Inc., Centennial, Colorado.

For more information about AccountingTools® products, visit our Web site at www.accountingtools.com.

ISBN-13: 978-1-938910-75-3

Printed in the United States of America

Table of Contents

Preface

Construction accounting applies to a large part of the economy, since it includes *any* type of construction, such as homes, office buildings, highways, pipelines, and power plants. There are a number of unique aspects to construction accounting that are not encountered in other industries, such as the accumulation of information by job, recognizing revenues and costs based on the percentage of completion (or other methods), and the treatment of change orders and claims. In *Construction Accounting*, we address every aspect of the accounting that one might encounter in a construction business. The intent is to not only explain accounting concepts, but also provide examples and show how an accounting system can be constructed and operated.

The book is divided into three sections. In Chapters 1 through 5, we cover the essential building blocks of construction accounting, including the chart of accounts, cost codes, the job cost and equipment ledgers, and the resulting financial statements. In Chapters 6 through 12, we address the specific accounting for a number of functional areas, including fixed assets, payables, debt, leases, and payroll. In Chapters 13 through 16, we address several related topics that are crucial to the operation of a construction business, including tax issues, controls, the analysis of specific jobs, and the alternative legal structures that can be used.

You can find the answers to many questions about construction accounting in the following chapters, including:

- What cost codes are used in a construction accounting system?
- How does a job cost ledger support a construction accounting system?
- When should the percentage of completion method be used?
- Which journal entries impact the job cost ledger?
- Which unique line items applicable to construction appear in the financial statements?
- What is the accounting for construction fixed assets?
- How does one account for an investment in a construction joint venture?
- Which tax issues are most applicable to contractors?
- Which analysis reports can be created to examine the performance of a job?

Construction Accounting is designed for the accountant who wants to set up and operate an accounting system that is specific to the needs of a contractor or similar enterprise.

Centennial, Colorado
October 2016

About the Author

Steven Bragg, CPA, has been the chief financial officer or controller of four companies, as well as a consulting manager at Ernst & Young. He received a master's degree in finance from Bentley College, an MBA from Babson College, and a Bachelor's degree in Economics from the University of Maine. He has been a two-time president of the Colorado Mountain Club, and is an avid alpine skier, mountain biker and certified master diver. Mr. Bragg resides in Centennial, Colorado. He has written the following books and courses:

7 Habits of Effective CFOs	Enterprise Risk Management
7 Habits of Effective Controllers	Fair Value Accounting
Accountants' Guidebook	Financial Analysis
Accounting Changes and Error Corrections	Financial Forecasting and Modeling
Accounting Controls Guidebook	Fixed Asset Accounting
Accounting for Casinos and Gaming	Foreign Currency Accounting
Accounting for Derivatives and Hedges	Fraud Examination
Accounting for Earnings per Share	GAAP Guidebook
Accounting for Inventory	Hospitality Accounting
Accounting for Investments	How to Run a Meeting
Accounting for Intangible Assets	Human Resources Guidebook
Accounting for Leases	IFRS Guidebook
Accounting for Managers	Interpretation of Financial Statements
Accounting for Stock-Based Compensation	Inventory Management
Accounting Procedures Guidebook	Investor Relations Guidebook
Agricultural Accounting	Lean Accounting Guidebook
Bookkeeping Guidebook	Mergers & Acquisitions
Budgeting	Negotiation
Business Combinations and Consolidations	New Controller Guidebook
Business Insurance Fundamentals	Nonprofit Accounting
Business Ratios	Partnership Accounting
Business Valuation	Payables Management
Capital Budgeting	Payroll Management
CFO Guidebook	Project Accounting
Change Management	Project Management
Closing the Books	Public Company Accounting
Coaching and Mentoring	Purchasing Guidebook
Constraint Management	Real Estate Accounting
Construction Accounting	Records Management
Corporate Cash Management	Recruiting and Hiring
Corporate Finance	Revenue Recognition
Cost Accounting (college textbook)	The MBA Guidebook
Cost Accounting Fundamentals	The Soft Close
Cost Management Guidebook	The Statement of Cash Flows
Credit & Collection Guidebook	The Year-End Close
Developing and Managing Teams	Treasurer's Guidebook
Employee Onboarding	Working Capital Management

On-Line Resources by Steven Bragg

Steven maintains the accountingtools.com web site, which contains continuing professional education courses, the Accounting Best Practices podcast, and hundreds of articles on accounting subjects.

Construction Accounting is also available as a continuing professional education (CPE) course. You can purchase the course (and many other courses) and take an on-line exam at:

www.accountingtools.com/cpe

Chapter 1
Overview of the Construction Industry

Introduction

The construction industry involves any activity that prepares land for use and creates or repairs buildings and other structures. According to the North American Industry Classification System (NAICS), the construction industry is comprised of the sub-classifications noted in the following table.

NAICS Codes for the Construction Industry

NAICS Code	Description
236115	New Single Family Housing Construction
236116	New Multifamily Housing Construction
236117	New Housing For-Sale Builders
236118	Residential Remodelers
236210	Industrial Building Construction
236220	Commercial and Institutional Building Construction
237110	Water and Sewer Line and Related Structures Construction
237120	Oil and Gas Pipeline and Related Structures Construction
237130	Power and Communication Line and Related Structures Construction
237210	Land Subdivision
237310	Highway, Street, and Bridge Construction
237990	Other Heavy and Civil Engineering Construction
238110	Poured Concrete Foundation and Structure Contractors
238120	Structural Steel and Precast Concrete Contractors
238130	Framing Contractors
238140	Masonry Contractors
238150	Glass and Glazing Contractors
238160	Roofing Contractors
238170	Siding Contractors
238190	Other Foundation, Structure, and Building Exterior Contractors
238210	Electrical Contractors and Other Wiring Installation Contractors
238220	Plumbing, Heating, and Air-Conditioning Contractors
238290	Other Building Equipment Contractors
238310	Drywall and Insulation Contractors
238320	Painting and Wall Covering Contractors
238330	Flooring Contractors
238340	Tile and Terrazzo Contractors

NAICS Code	Description
238350	Finish Carpentry Contractors
238390	Other Building Finishing Contractors
238910	Site Preparation Contractors
238990	All Other Specialty Trade Contractors

As of 2016, the United States Census Bureau estimated that the annual revenue of the construction industry in the United States was $1.6 trillion, which was earned by more than 729,000 construction companies. In short, the construction industry is one of the most important and broad-based sectors of the economy. Given its importance, it should be no surprise that there are unique accounting requirements related to the construction industry, which we delve into later in this book. In this chapter, we address the types of work engaged in by a construction contractor, the bidding and construction process, the types of construction contracts, and several related topics mostly pertaining to the difficulty of operating within this industry.

Nature of the Construction Contractor

Most construction contractors are highly specialized, engaging in only a few sub-disciplines within the construction field (as indicated by the many NAICS codes for the construction industry). The bulk of the industry is comprised of quite small construction companies that operate solely within small geographic areas. Only a few firms have gathered sufficient mass to be able to compete successfully for billion-dollar or international projects. This disparity, with so many small contractors, is likely due to the ease with which individuals can enter the field, requiring little capital to get started.

A contractor may follow one of three routes when engaging in construction activities. These alternatives are:

- *General contractor.* In this role, the entity is the prime contractor who commits to complete a project for a client and who is responsible for its completion. The general contractor may engage the services of a number of subcontractors to ensure that work is completed.
- *Subcontractor.* In this role, the entity provides specialized services for a phase of the total project to either the general contractor or another contractor that is positioned between the subcontractor and the general contractor.
- *Construction manager.* In this role, the entity acts on behalf of the owner of a project to supervise all construction activity. The construction manager may also negotiate contracts with other parties for the construction work.

A construction company does not sell goods or services to customers in the manner found in most other industries, where there is no need for a formal contract. In the construction industry, the outcome is usually customized and involves a significant expenditure by the client. Because of these conditions, there is nearly always a formal contract between the parties, delineating the work to be performed, what constitutes completion of the contract to the satisfaction of the client, and the compensation to be paid.

The resulting work usually extends across multiple reporting periods, which makes it difficult to track and report on job-related revenues and costs within any one reporting period.

Bonding Requirements

A unique aspect of the construction industry is that clients may require contractors to post a bond that protects them against any failure by the contractor to meet the clients' performance or payment requirements. The following are different types of bonds:

- A *bid bond* requires a contractor to pay the difference between the contractor's bid and the bid of the next lowest bidder, in the event that the contractor does not sign the contract with the client. The intent is to protect the client from bidders that do not have the resources to complete the work associated with a project; the amount of the bond acts as a threshold that bars financially weak companies from bidding.
- A *payment bond* is an amount used as a guarantee that the contractor will pay its employees, suppliers, and subcontractors. Otherwise, these entities could attach liens against the client's project in the amounts payable to them.
- A *performance bond* is used to reimburse the client if the contractor is unable to complete a project; the funds can then be used to pay a different contractor to complete the work.

Governments are required by law to impose bonding rules on contractors, while commercial clients may do so at their discretion. These bonds may be provided by surety companies, which make themselves liable for the performance of a contractor. A surety company examines the financial statements of a contractor in detail before agreeing to post a bond on the contractor's behalf. Because of this need for surety firms to fully understand the finances of contractors, they are one of the most frequent users of financial statements within the industry.

Bonding requirements can be so onerous that several contractors may elect to combine their resources into a joint venture arrangement. A joint venture allows several smaller contractors to bid on larger jobs. In addition, they can combine their unique skill sets in this arrangement, allowing them to win bids that they could not obtain if they were to bid individually. When a joint venture arrangement is used, the parties to it create an agreement that states how profits, losses, and risks will be shared among the group. We discuss the accounting for joint ventures in the Investments in Construction Joint Ventures chapter.

The Bidding and Construction Process

A contractor does not start work on a project until a detailed estimation and bidding process has been completed. The usual estimation and bidding process flow for a larger project is as follows:

1. The owner of the property hires an architect, whose role at this stage is to prepare preliminary plans and cost estimates. The owner reviews this information and decides whether it is worthwhile to proceed. If so, the architect is instructed to prepare more detailed information that can be used as part of a bidding process.

2. The owner contacts one or more general contractors, asking for bids. The owner sends bid packets to those contractors expressing interest in the project. Bonding requirements may be used at this stage to limit the pool of potential bidders.

3. Each contractor's estimating department compiles the costs it believes will be incurred to meet the owner's requirements. These estimates take into consideration the types and quantities of materials needed, the different labor skill levels required, and the types of equipment that will be needed. Further estimating considerations are:

   a. Each contractor decides how to obtain or finance the equipment that will be needed on a job. This may involve purchasing, renting, or leasing the equipment, as well as consideration of the financing that will be needed for each decision. These decisions are built into the bid proposal.

   b. Each contractor turns to its subcontractors and asks them to prepare bids for their areas of specialization on the project. These subcontractors may in turn ask for bids from their subcontractors. These layers of bid submissions can significantly delay submission of the final bid to the owner of the property.

4. Once all costs have been compiled, the contractors decide upon the amount of markup they will charge on the labor, material, subcontractor, and equipment costs. The estimating team will need to consider many factors, such as the difficulty it has had in the past in dealing with the owner, its need for more work, the contractor's level of experience with this type of work, and the level of complexity of the work.

5. Once the cost and profit information has been assembled, the team estimates the timing and amount of cash flows that will result from the project. Based on this information, the total price is allocated among the various job elements to ensure that enough cash is received from the owner at regular intervals to support the expenditures required by the project.

6. The owner then receives all bids, compares the various offerings, and selects a bidder as the winner. This may or may not be the low bidder; for example, if a certain bidder is known to have particular expertise in the owner's project area, the owner may select that bidder even if it has submitted a significantly higher bid.

7. The parties sign a contract, after which work begins. There may be additional negotiations through the entire work period as the owner requests changes and the contractor submits change orders that accommodate the requested changes.
8. The selected contractor's purchasing department issues purchase orders for the requisite materials, while also entering into contracts with those subcontractors selected for the job.
9. The contractor sets up the job site. This may include the construction of a temporary field office, positioning equipment on the site and running temporary power lines to the site.
10. The accounting staff sets up a separate job in the job cost ledger, along with a set of cost codes to which incoming billings will be charged. For efficiency purposes, a standard set of cost codes are initially loaded into the job cost ledger for the job; some of these codes will be deactivated if there are no corresponding cost categories in the job budget.
11. The contractor begins work on the job site.

We have just referred to several new concepts – the job cost ledger and cost codes. We will describe these concepts in the Construction Accounting System chapter.

Types of Construction Contracts

There are three types of contracts than a contractor can enter into with a client. Each type has specific characteristics that tend to favor one party or the other, depending on the circumstances. We explain each one in the following sub-sections.

Fixed Fee Contract

A fixed fee contract is used when the contractor commits to being paid a fixed amount by the client. In this situation, the costs incurred by the contractor have no impact on the price paid. This arrangement would appear to strongly favor the client, since there is no risk of paying more than the contract price. In fact, this arrangement is most common in a multi-party bidding scenario where a number of potential contractors are forced to bid against each other. However, there are two situations in which a fixed fee arrangement could favor the contractor; they are:

- *Low-cost producer*. The contractor may believe it can meet the client's requirements without incurring a significant cost overrun, and so feels comfortable in setting a price that will yield an unusually large profit. This can result in unethical behavior to minimize costs incurred to the point where the project outcome barely meets the quality standards of the client.
- *Contract additions*. The contractor goes into the arrangement with the intent of creating additions to the contract whenever the client's specifications increase beyond the baseline established in the original contract. In this manner, the contractor expects to earn a profit from change orders.

It is best from the perspectives of both the client and contractor to create quite detailed specifications for a fixed fee contract, so there is little question about what is expected of the contractor and what constitutes an acceptable final outcome.

Cost Plus Contract

A cost plus contract is a cost-based method for setting the price of a construction project under a contractual arrangement. The contractor adds together the direct material cost, direct labor cost, and overhead costs for a project and adds to it a markup percentage in order to derive the price to be billed. From the client's perspective, this can be an expensive pricing system, since costs may spiral well above initial expectations. However, it is an ideal system when there is a high degree of uncertainty regarding the design specifications of the final product.

A client is more likely to use this type of contract when its primary concerns are with the perceived capability and reliability of the contractor, rather than with the ultimate cost of the contract. There is a reduced need to identify the precise deliverables as part of the initial contract. Instead, the contractor may be asked to develop the project specifications in conjunction with the client once the contract has been awarded.

EXAMPLE

Cantilever Construction is bidding on a project that is expected to contain the following costs:

Material costs	$1,120,000
Labor costs	550,000
Allocated overhead	215,000
Total costs	$1,885,000

Under the terms of the proposed contract, the company is allowed to add a 10% markup to all of its costs. To derive the estimated revenues to be gained from this contract, Cantilever adds together the stated costs to arrive at a total cost of $1,885,000 and then multiplies this amount by $(1 + 0.10)$ to arrive at the total contract price of $2,073,500.

The following are advantages of using the cost plus pricing method:
- *Simple.* It is quite easy to derive a bid price using this method, though it is necessary to define the overhead allocation method for costs that can be assigned to the project.
- *Assured contract profits.* Any contractor is willing to accept this method for a contractual arrangement with a client, since it is assured of having its costs reimbursed and of making a profit. There is no risk of loss on such a contract.

However, from the perspective of any client that hires a contractor under a cost plus pricing arrangement, the contractor has no incentive to curtail its expenditures - on the contrary, it will likely include as many costs as possible in the contract so that it can be reimbursed. To combat this issue, a contractual arrangement may include cost-reduction incentives for the contractor.

Unit-Price Contract

A unit-price contract is an arrangement in which the client pays a specific price for each unit of output. This arrangement is rarely used in a large, complex construction project where there are few units of output that are easily replicated. For example, a client is unlikely to demand a unit-price contract for each of a cluster of apartment buildings. However, the general contractor may use this type of contract with its subcontractors for selected work arrangements. For example, a general contractor for the construction of a road could enter into a unit-price contract that pays a certain amount per square foot of sidewalk installed.

Construction Contract Modifiers

Any of the preceding contract types may have modifying clauses built into them, which can be used to alter the risks assumed by the two parties. Examples of these clauses are:
- *Guaranteed maximum.* The client seeks to keep the total cost of the contract from exceeding a certain amount. This clause can be a difficult one for the contractor to accept, since it implies that the client will not impose too many scope changes once the initial contract has been signed. If a large number of scope changes are requested, the contractor is likely to demand a renegotiation of the guaranteed maximum price.
- *Overrun cost sharing.* In a cost plus arrangement, the contractor has no incentive to reduce its costs by targeting efficiencies. The client can demand an overrun cost sharing clause in order to incentivize the contractor to manage its costs more effectively. Under this arrangement, a portion of each cost overrun must be absorbed by the contractor, rather than being automatically passed through to the client.
- *Underrun profit sharing.* If costs are not as high as expected, the contractor does not fare as well under a cost plus contract, since its profit will be reduced. The client can offer to mitigate this effect by splitting some portion of the cost savings with the contractor.
- *Overrun penalty.* The client may want a threshold cost target, above which it sets a significant penalty that the contractor will incur. This approach can also be targeted at a non-cost performance item, such as a penalty for every extra hour that a bridge construction project closes down a major highway.
- *Early delivery bonus.* If the client must obtain use of the final product as early as possible, it can offer an early delivery bonus. This bonus may be structured to increase in size for an exceedingly early delivery, in order to

provide a large incentive for the contractor to use its best project planning staff.

Contract Changes

When a project involves billing a client under a fixed fee arrangement, there is a strong likelihood that the scope of the project will change over time, especially when the project is quite complex. For example, there may be changes in the design of the project, the materials to be used, or the completion due date. These changes can result in change orders, claims and back charges, which are explained in this section.

When there are project changes, it will be necessary for the contractor and the client to mutually agree upon a change order that specifies the extent of the scope change, as well as the related alteration in the amount that the contractor is now allowed to bill to the client. There can be a number of disputes over change orders, especially when they are being authorized by different representatives of the client who are not coordinating their actions. The end result is that there can be prolonged disputes over the final billing amount that the client will pay, which makes it difficult to determine the profitability of a job.

There are cases in which a change order is unpriced – that is, the parties have agreed to a change, but there has been no formal agreement regarding how the change impacts the price that the client will pay.

A contract claim is an amount in excess of the contract price that a contractor is attempting to collect from the client. There are a number of possible causes for contract claims, including the following:

- Change orders that are currently being disputed
- Delays in the construction schedule caused by the client
- Errors in the plans provided by the client
- The termination of a contract

A back charge is a billing for work performed or costs incurred by one party that should have been incurred by the party being billed. For example, the owner of a project finds that the site required extensive cleaning following the departure of all work crews. This cleaning was the responsibility of the general contractor, so the owner back charges the general contractor for the cleanup cost.

Construction Industry Failure Issues

Construction companies are very likely to fail, because the nature of the business requires close attention to costs incurred and the financing of the organization. There are several unique aspects to the construction industry that make it more difficult to successfully run a business. These issues are:

- *Unique projects.* Each construction project is unique, so the accounting for it cannot be standardized. For example, a construction company could be involved with the construction of an office building, a residential home, a bridge, and a dam.

- *Cost differences*. Even when a set of projects appear to be quite similar (such as a series of identical residential homes), there are still cost differences based on site conditions and locations. For example, a series of downpours followed by flooding can damage a structure and greatly delay its completion. Or, the use of identical architectural drawings to construct two homes that are 20 miles apart can result in different costs, because of differing labor rates and equipment rental charges.

- *Fixed fee bids*. A construction company may make a fixed fee bid for a project in order to remove the risk of cost overruns from the customer. Of course, this means that the company is taking on the risk of cost overruns. These cost overruns could be substantial, especially when the company has limited experience with the project in question and does not have a history of buying from the local group of suppliers and subcontractors.

- *Variable demand*. A construction company may face prolonged gaps in the demand for its services, which makes it difficult to support a full-time staff. When there is a shortfall in demand, it may be necessary to lay off large numbers of employees. Or, to keep them employed, the bidding team may bid low to win contracts, even though doing so eliminates the bulk of the profits from a project. A worst-case scenario is to engage in speculative projects, where there is no apparent buyer at the start of a project. The company may use up a large part of its available financing to fund speculative projects and then may have to modify the final product before a buyer will be willing to purchase it.

- *Shifting resource assignments*. A business may have a number of construction sites open at any one time. This means that resources can bounce around among the sites as they are needed. For example, a group of plumbers may move between three job sites in one week. When resources are shifting around so much, it is easy for some projects to accumulate excessive costs without anyone noticing.

- *Uncertain payments*. A construction contractor incurs substantial costs for building materials and labor, which are paid for by client payments that can have uncertain timing. If a client is even a few days or weeks late in making a payment, this can have a profoundly negative impact on cash flows. Further, clients may retain a portion of these payments until the project is both complete and approved. If a project is delayed for any reason, so too are these retention payments.

Given the preceding issues, a firm in the construction business needs to pay great attention to its cost estimating process, the costs it is incurring, and the timing of cash flows.

Summary

Though there are a great many companies operating within the construction industry, it is one of the more difficult areas in which to consistently turn a profit.

The use of competitive bidding, the level of conflict over change orders, and the shifting levels of demand can seriously impact profits unless company management is exceedingly careful to monitor project results. The foundation of this analysis work is the accounting system, which collects and aggregates financial information into a format that can then be used to run a construction business. We explore the structure of this accounting system and its outputs in the following chapters.

Chapter 2
The Construction Accounting System

Introduction

A construction company requires an unusually broad-based accounting system that has a strong set of features in regard to information storage, purchasing, billings, payables, and change order tracking. These features are needed to keep track of the massive amount of information that is collected for each job, deal with retainages from clients and to subcontractors, address the ongoing flurry of change orders, and keep track of the multitude of purchases associated with jobs.

In this chapter, we deal with all of the preceding issues, but mostly concentrate on the information storage requirement. This topic covers the chart of accounts, general ledger, and several ledgers that roll up into the general ledger.

Nature of a Construction Accounting System

The accounting systems used by a construction business can be exceptionally complex or relatively simple, depending on the size and scope of its operations. However, they all share the same functionality, which is described in this section.

It is possible to rent an online "software as a service" (SAAS) construction accounting system, where the accounting software is maintained and updated by a third party. However, most construction companies still maintain their own in-house accounting systems. This means that they have purchased construction accounting software, stored it on a server, and have made it accessible to multiple employees from their own workstations. The functionality of these two types of systems is the same and encompasses the following essential features:

- *Chart of accounts.* The system has a standard set of accounts that are usable by a construction company, which can be expanded upon with additional accounts as needed. A sample chart of accounts appears in a later section.
- *Ledgers.* The system should use three ledgers to store transaction information. These ledgers are the general ledger, job cost ledger, and equipment ledger. The general ledger is the primary ledger in which transactional information is stored and from which the financial statements are compiled. It is described in more detail in a later section. The job cost ledger is a subsidiary ledger in which job-specific transactional information is stored. The equipment ledger is also a subsidiary ledger, and is used to store transactional information about vehicles and heavy equipment. The information in the two subsidiary ledgers is copied forward at a summary level to the general ledger. It is essential for a construction company to have a separate job cost ledger. An equipment ledger is only necessary when the firm has a significant investment in fixed assets.

- *Job cost tracking.* As noted in the earlier ledgers requirement, the system should track costs at the individual job level. This means reporting all costs that can be assigned to a job, including labor costs, materials costs, equipment costs, subcontractor costs, and assigned overhead costs.
- *Purchase orders.* The system allows for the entry of purchase orders that state which costs have been committed to a project, even if suppliers have not yet issued invoices to the company. This feature is separate from the accounting system in other industries, but is a critical part of the system in the construction industry, since it allows the accountant to report on committed costs. With this information, managers will know if a project is in danger of losing money and still have time to take remedial action.
- *Payables.* The system is used to record incoming invoices from suppliers and subcontractors, schedules them for payment, and issues electronic or check payments when the due date is reached. The system should be able to deduct retainage amounts from payments to subcontractors, which are to be paid at a later date.
- *Change order tracking.* Whenever there is a change to the original construction plan, this alters the amount of costs that will be incurred and the company can (hopefully) bill the client for an additional amount related to this change. Change order tracking is a feature not normally found in accounting systems designed for general use in other industries.
- *Billings.* The system is used to create invoices for clients and record the related receivables. When cash is received from clients, the cash is logged against the outstanding receivables, which reduces the amount of unpaid receivables.
- *Asset tracking.* The system tracks the cost of all fixed assets owned by the company and depreciates them at a standard rate over their useful lives.
- *Financial statements.* The system accumulates all of the general ledger account information into a standard set of financial statements, which are comprised of the income statement, balance sheet, and statement of cash flows. These statements are described further in the Construction Financial Statements chapter.
- *Project reporting.* The system reports on the costs and billings accumulated against each individual project. Ideally, the system should be able to report on just the unfavorable variances for a project, so that managers are not swamped with an excessive amount of detail. Examples of the reports that the system could generate are:
    - Supplier and contractor billings to the company that exceed the amount of the authorizing purchase order
    - Hours charged to a job that exceed the planned amount
- *Tax forms.* The system flags suppliers as being eligible to receive the year-end Form 1099, and then accumulates the information needed to prepare the form.

In the preceding list of system features, we noted that committed costs should be tracked in order to estimate the profitability of a construction project. A committed cost arises in any situation in which the company guarantees that it will pay a third party.

EXAMPLE

Jones Construction commits to pay $10,000 to Ditch Wizards once they complete the excavation of a ditch that will be used to hide a water filtration system. This is a committed cost.

The Chart of Accounts

The chart of accounts is a listing of all accounts used in the general ledger, usually sorted in order by account number. The accounts are typically numeric, but can also be alphabetic or alphanumeric. The account numbering system is used by the accounting software to aggregate information into a firm's financial statements.

Accounts are usually listed in order of their appearance in the financial statements, starting with the balance sheet and continuing with the income statement. Thus, the chart of accounts begins with cash, proceeds through liabilities and shareholders' equity, and then continues with accounts for revenues and then expenses. Typical accounts found in the chart of accounts include the following:

Assets (items of economic value that are expected to yield a benefit in future periods)

- *Cash.* Contains the amounts of petty cash and bank account balances. There is usually a separate account for each bank account and a separate account for all petty cash.
- *Accounts receivable – trade.* Contains the balances of trade receivables, which are billings issued to clients. Trade receivables arise when clients promise to pay as of a later date.
- *Accounts receivable – retention.* Contains the amount of receivables designated as retention by clients. These receivables are paid at the end of a project. It is useful to separate this information from the trade receivables account for cash forecasting purposes, since the retention receivables will be paid to the company later.
- *Allowance for doubtful accounts.* Contains a reserve against expected future losses on accounts receivable. The account has a negative balance.
- *Marketable securities.* Contains the valuations of any investments that the company has made in marketable securities. In a smaller business, excess funds may be kept in a savings account at the bank, in which case these funds appear in a cash account.

- *Inventory*. Contains the cost of all building materials that have not yet been used. Construction companies tend to have relatively small investments in inventory.
- *Costs and profits in excess of billings*. Contains any excess of costs incurred by the business that have not yet been billed to clients, along with the associated profits. This account is used when a company employs the percentage of completion method, where estimated profits are recognized over the course of a project, rather than at its completion. If the cash method or the accrual method of accounting (as explained in the Construction-Specific Accounting chapter) is used, then this account is not needed.

> **Tip:** If a company is using the completed contract method to recognize revenue, the "costs and profits in excess of billings" account is instead labeled "costs in excess of billings."

- *Notes receivable*. Contains the amount of any notes from clients or other parties that are payable to the company within the next year.
- *Prepaid expenses*. Contains the unconsumed balances of any payments made, such as prepaid rent and prepaid insurance.
- *Other current assets*. This is a catchall account that contains all other assets that will be liquidated within one year.
- *Fixed assets*. Contains the amounts paid for fixed assets, such as buildings, construction equipment, office equipment and vehicles. These are assets that are expected to provide value to the company for multiple periods. This account may be subdivided into a separate account for each classification of fixed asset.
- *Accumulated depreciation*. Contains the grand total accumulation of depreciation charged against fixed assets over time. This account has a negative balance and offsets the amount of fixed assets. The fixed asset accounts and the accumulated depreciation account may be combined, resulting in a net fixed assets figure.
- *Intangible assets*. Contains the purchase costs of non-tangible assets, such as purchased patents, licenses, organization costs, and copyrights.
- *Other assets*. Contains all other assets that do not fit into the descriptions for the preceding asset accounts, and which are not expected to be liquidated within the next year.

Most of the preceding assets are considered to be current assets, which means that they will be liquidated within one year. If an asset is to be held longer than one year, it is considered a long-term asset. The one exception that may impact contractors is that assets can still be classified as current assets if they fall within the operating cycle of the business. An operating cycle is the time period from when cash is paid to acquire assets to the date when cash is received from selling the assets. A contractor may find that some of its contracts are substantially longer than one year, so the assets and liabilities related to those contracts could be classified as current assets or current liabilities, respectively. All other assets and liabilities not related to contracts will likely fall under the one-year rule for the purpose of classifying them.

Liabilities (an obligation payable to another entity or person)

- *Accounts payable – trade*. Contains the complete set of all payables owed to suppliers and subcontractors, based on invoices submitted by them.
- *Accounts payable – retention*. Contains that portion of all supplier and subcontractor invoices that the company is retaining until a project is complete. It is useful to separate this information from the trade payables account for cash forecasting purposes, since the retention payables will be paid later.
- *Billings in excess of costs and profits*. Contains any excess of billings issued over the costs incurred on client projects, along with the associated profits. This account is used when a company employs the percentage of completion method, where estimated profits are recognized over the course of a project, rather than at its completion. If the cash method or the accrual method of accounting (as explained in the Construction-Specific Accounting chapter) is used, then this account is not needed.

Tip: If a company is using the completed contract method to recognize revenue, the "billings in excess of costs and profits" account is instead labeled "billings in excess of costs."

- *Notes payable*. Contains the current balance of any notes payable to a third party and which will be paid off within the next year.
- *Accrued expenses*. Contains estimated liabilities for which no documented supplier or subcontractor invoices have yet been received. This account can also include unpaid wages to employees.
- *Warranty reserves*. Contains a reserve for the amount that the company expects to pay out for warranty claims. This amount is usually estimated based on past experience with similar projects.
- *Other current liabilities*. Contains all other liabilities that do not fit into one of the prior categories (such as taxes payable) and which the company expects to pay within the next year.
- *Long-term notes payable*. Contains the remaining balances of loans owed to lenders that will not be paid within the next year. There may be a separate account for each loan owed, so that payments are not confused among the different loans.

Most of the preceding liabilities are considered to be current liabilities, which means that they will be settled within one year. If a liability will not be paid for more than one year, it is considered a long-term liability.

Stockholders' Equity (the claims of owners on the residual assets of a business after liabilities have been paid)

- *Capital stock.* This account is used by corporations, which issue shares. It contains the amount of funds received by a business in exchange for the sale of its stock to investors. The amount recorded in this account is only the par value of each share. Par value is the legal capital per share, and is printed on the face of a stock certificate.
- *Additional paid-in capital.* Contains any additional amounts paid to the organization by an investor for shares in the business that exceed the par value of the shares.
- *Retained earnings.* Contains the accumulated amount of any earnings generated by a business that have not been distributed to shareholders.

Revenue (an increase in assets or decrease in liabilities caused by the provision of services or products to customers)

- *Revenue.* Contains the gross amount of all sales recognized during the reporting period. Sales are recognized in different amounts and with different timing, depending on the type of revenue recognition method used.

Expenses (the reduction in value of an asset as it is used to generate revenue)

- *Cost of construction.* Contains the cost of all materials, labor, subcontractors, equipment, and other items. These costs can be traced to a specific project. Each of these expenses may be substantial, and so are commonly tracked in separate accounts. Additional points related to these costs are:
  - *Materials.* The cost of materials includes the cost to transport the items to the building site, its storage once it has been purchased, and any applicable sales or other taxes.
  - *Labor.* The cost of labor includes the employer's share of all payroll taxes and benefits.
  - *Subcontractors.* The cost of subcontractors includes all subcontractors paid through the company's accounts payable system. This cost likely includes both the materials and labor supplied by the subcontractors, so it is really a blend of the preceding two expense items.
  - *Equipment.* The cost of equipment is those costs associated with construction equipment that can be directly associated with a project. This charge may come from rented equipment (where the rental fee is charged to the job) or from owned equipment (where the equipment depreciation or a usage fee is charged to the job).
  - *Other items.* The cost of other items frequently includes services provided by a third party, such as surveying fees and the rental and servicing of portable toilets at job sites.

- *Advertising and promotions.* Contains the recognized cost of advertising expenditures and other types of promotions used to make prospective clients aware of the company and its services.
- *Bank fees.* Contains the fees charged by a company's bank to process transactions and maintain bank accounts.
- *Benefits.* Contains the cost of all types of employee benefits paid for by the company, such as health care, life insurance, and disability insurance.
- *Charitable contributions.* Contains the cost of all contributions made by the company; the account includes expenditures that match employee donations.
- *Depreciation.* Contains a depreciation charge that reflects the consumption of fixed assets over time.
- *Dues and memberships.* Contains the cost of all membership fees paid by the organization.
- *Fuel and lubrication.* Contains the costs of the fuel and other liquids needed to maintain the company's vehicles and other equipment. This account may be merged into one of the cost of goods sold accounts.
- *Insurance.* Contains the cost of all business insurance. The costs of benefits described as "insurance" are recorded in the Benefits account.
- *Interest.* Includes the debt cost on all outstanding loans. Related loan fees are typically included in this account.
- *Janitorial expenses.* Contains the cost of all cleaning services incurred by the company.
- *Office rent.* Contains the cost of the rent associated with the facilities used by the business. The rental of equipment may be allocated to the cost of goods sold, if it relates to construction activities.
- *Office supplies.* Contains the cost of all supplies consumed by the business. When supplies are purchased, they are usually assumed to have been consumed at that point.
- *Postage and delivery.* Contains all delivery charges, such as overnight mail, normal postage and courier services.
- *Professional fees.* Contains the fees charged by outside administrative and legal services, such as auditor fees and attorney fees.
- *Repairs and maintenance.* Contains the cost of repairs and maintenance for the administrative side of the business.
- *Salaries and wages.* Includes only the cost of compensation for people not associated with construction projects; project-related compensation is charged to the cost of goods sold.
- *Taxes and licenses.* Contains the government fees charged to the administrative side of the business. If these fees relate to a specific project, they are instead charged to the cost of goods sold.
- *Telephones.* Contains the periodic charges associated with land lines and cell phones.
- *Training.* Contains the out-of-pocket cost of all employee training.

- *Travel and entertainment.* Contains the costs of employee travel, including airfare, taxis, hotels, dining, and related expenditures.
- *Utilities.* Contains the aggregated cost of all utilities, which may include water, heat, electricity, waste disposal, and so forth.
- *Warranty expense.* Contains the periodic charge for the amount that the company expects to pay out for warranty claims; this charge is used to build up the warranty reserve.
- *Other income.* Contains income from a variety of incidental sources that are individually too small to warrant the use of a separate account. This is usually income from activities unrelated to the core construction activities of the business.
- *Other expenses.* Contains a variety of incidental expenses that are individually too small to warrant the use of a separate account.
- *Income taxes.* Contains the amount charged to expense for the company's income tax liability.

A three-digit chart of accounts allows a business to create a numerical sequence of accounts that can contain as many as 1,000 potential accounts. The three-digit format is most commonly used by small businesses that do not break out the results of any departments in their financial statements. A sample three-digit chart of accounts is shown below.

Sample Three-Digit Chart of Accounts

Account Number	Description
100	Cash
110	Accounts receivable – trade
115	Accounts receivable – retention
116	Allowance for doubtful accounts
120	Marketable securities
130	Inventory
140	Costs and profits in excess of billings
150	Notes receivable
160	Prepaid expenses
170	Other current assets
200	Fixed assets – buildings
210	Fixed assets – construction equipment
220	Fixed assets – office equipment
230	Fixed assets – vehicles
235	Accumulated depreciation
240	Other assets
300	Accounts payable - trade
305	Accounts payable – retention
310	Billings in excess of costs and profits

Account Number	Description
320	Notes payable
330	Accrued expenses
340	Warranty reserves
350	Other current liabilities
360	Long-term notes payable
400	Capital stock
410	Additional paid-in capital
420	Retained earnings
500	Revenue
600	Cost of construction – materials
610	Cost of construction – labor
620	Cost of construction – subcontractors
630	Cost of construction – equipment
640	Cost of construction – other
700	Advertising and promotions
702	Bank fees
704	Benefits
706	Charitable contributions
708	Depreciation
710	Dues and memberships
712	Fuel and lubrication
714	Insurance
716	Interest expense
718	Janitorial expenses
720	Office rent
722	Office supplies
724	Postage and delivery
726	Professional fees
728	Repairs and maintenance
730	Salaries and wages
732	Taxes and licenses
734	Telephones
736	Training
738	Travel and entertainment
740	Utilities
742	Warranty expense
800	Other income
810	Other expenses
820	Income taxes

In the example, each block of related accounts begins with a different set of account numbers. Thus, current liabilities begin with "300," revenue items begin with "500," and cost of goods sold items begin with "600." This numbering scheme makes it easier for the accountant to remember where accounts are located within the chart of accounts. Also, the accounts numbered from "100" to "420" are aggregated into the balance sheet, while accounts numbered "500" to "820" are aggregated into the income statement. This type of account range format is also required by the report writing module in many accounting software packages.

> **Tip:** As shown in the preceding example, leave plenty of room in the numbering assigned to accounts, so that additional accounts can be inserted between existing accounts at a later date.

The General Ledger

A general ledger is the master set of accounts in which is summarized all transactions occurring within a business during a specific period of time. The general ledger contains all of the accounts currently being used in a chart of accounts and is sorted by account number. Either individual transactions or summary-level postings from subsidiary ledgers are listed within each account number, and are sorted by transaction date. Each entry in the general ledger includes a reference number that states the source of the information. The source may be a subsidiary ledger, a journal entry (as described in the Construction Transactions chapter), or a transaction entered directly into the general ledger.

The format of the general ledger varies somewhat, depending on the accounting software being used, but the basic set of information presented for an account within the general ledger is:

- *Transaction number.* The software assigns a unique number to each transaction, so that it can be more easily located in the accounting database if you know the transaction number.
- *Transaction date.* This is the date on which the transaction was entered into the accounting database.
- *Description.* This is a brief description that summarizes the reason for the entry.
- *Source.* Information may be forwarded to the general ledger from a variety of sources, so the report should state the source, in case it is necessary to go back to the source to research the reason for the entry.
- *Debit and credit.* States the amount debited or credited to the account for a specific transaction.

The following sample of a general ledger report shows a possible format that could be used to present information for several transactions that are aggregated under a specific account number.

Sample General Ledger Presentation

Trans. No.	Trans. Date	Description	Source	Debit	Credit
Acct. 706		**Acct: Charitable Contributions**	**Beginning balance**		**$7,500.00**
10473	3/22/xx	Petty cash contribution	JE	50.00	
10474	3/23/xx	Supplier invoice	AP	200.00	
10475	3/24/xx	Contribution from expense report	AP	100.00	
10476	3/25/xx	Supplier invoice	AP	400.00	
18903	3/26/xx	Matching of employee contribution	JE	50.00	
			Ending balance		**$8,300.00**

It is extremely easy to locate information pertinent to an accounting inquiry in the general ledger, which makes it the primary source of accounting information. For example:

- A manager reviews the balance sheet and notices that the amount of debt appears too high. The accountant looks up the debt account in the general ledger and sees that a loan was added at the end of the month.
- A manager reviews the income statement and sees that the bad debt expense is very high. The accountant looks up the expense in the general ledger, drills down to the source journal entry, and sees that a new bad debt projection was the cause of the increase in bad debt expense.

As the examples show, the source of an inquiry is frequently the financial statements; when conducting an investigation, the accountant begins with the general ledger and may drill down to source documents from there to ascertain the reason(s) for an issue.

The Work Breakdown Structure

Some projects are inordinately large, making them quite difficult to manage. This issue can be addressed by employing the work breakdown structure, which identifies every task in a project. This process of identification breaks down a project into a cluster of bite-sized pieces that are easier to manage. Each task is listed in an outline format, so that a great many tasks can be clearly stated within a relatively small document. With this information in hand, one can more easily do the following:

- Clearly state all aspects of a project's scope
- Monitor the completion stage of each identified task
- Compile the cost of each task
- Develop work assignments for each task

From an accounting perspective, the key use of a work breakdown structure is to use it as the basis for an account coding system in the job cost ledger (which is described in the following section).

The work breakdown structure of a project divides activities into *summary tasks* and *work packages*. A summary task describes a set of activities (work packages). A work package is a group of activities for which work is estimated, scheduled, monitored, and controlled. A work package defines work at the lowest level for which cost and duration can be estimated and managed. For example, constructing a shed is a summary task, while laying the foundation, constructing a frame, and building a roof are all work packages within the summary task.

When all of the work packages are complete, the summary task is also accomplished. A sample work breakdown structure for the construction of a new home appears in the following exhibit.

Sample Work Breakdown Structure for a Home Construction Project

1.0 Design building structure

2.0 Lay foundation
    2.1 Dig hole
    2.2 Build concrete forms
    2.3 Pour concrete

3.0 Construct home
    3.1 Construct frame
    3.2 Add exterior walls
    3.3 Add plumbing
    3.4 Add wiring
    3.5 Add interior walls
    3.6 Add roof
    3.7 Add carpeting and hardwood floors
    3.8 Add windows

4.0 Install lawn
    4.1 Dig trenches
        4.1.1 Have the local utility mark all gas lines
        4.1.2. Identify trench lines
        4.1.3 Rent trench digging equipment
        4.1.4 Dig trenches
    4.2 Install sprinkler pipes
    4.3 Cover sprinkler system
    4.4 Plant lawn seed
    4.5 Plant shrubs

In the preceding exhibit, the top-level activities (noted in bold) are the summary tasks. These are known as *level one* items. All of the indented activities are the work packages. The indented activities can be indented further to denote additional levels of detail, as we noted for the "dig trenches" work package. In that work package,

"Dig trenches" was a *level two* item, while "Have the local utility mark all gas lines" was a *level three* item. These extra levels of detail are useful for providing a high level of refinement to a project.

The easiest way to construct a work breakdown structure is to start with the highest-level tasks that are required for a project and list them as top-tier items (summary tasks). Then list all tasks required to complete each summary task.

When creating a work breakdown structure, follow these best practices to improve the odds that the outcome properly reflects the actual project:

- Does the summary task matter? The costs of the work packages underneath a summary task are aggregated at the summary task level. Will anyone review this summary-level information or be responsible for it? If not, try reconfiguring to arrive at a more meaningful summary task.

- Should a work package be linked to a certain summary task? Verify that all work packages are actually associated with the summary task under which they are listed. If not, move the work packages under a more applicable summary task.

- Does a work package result in a product? There should be a specific outcome associated with each work package. Thus, "evaluate subcontractors" is not a work package, since there may be no end to this activity. Instead, use "select a subcontractor," which implies that there is a solid outcome to the activity.

- Is a work package too large? When a task is estimated to require a massive number of hours, the daily monitoring of the work does not tell the project manager if there is any real progress. Instead, many hours may pass before anyone realizes that there is a problem. To correct this problem, break the work package down into smaller segments that can be more easily tracked on a daily basis. As a general rule, try to restrict all work packages to no more than two weeks.

> **Tip:** No work package should be scheduled to span a period longer than the interval between two status meetings. Thus, if status meetings are 10 days apart, the work package limit should also be 10 days. By doing so, the status report for any work package should not involve an amorphous percentage of completion for more than one meeting.

- Has the work breakdown structure been stated at too fine a level of detail? When there are too many work packages for a large project, this may result in thousands of charge codes, which take time to set up and monitor.

- Is it too difficult to estimate the duration of a work package? If so, chop the package into smaller segments and try again. Smaller work packages are easier to estimate.

The Job Cost Ledger

A key element of a construction company's accounting system is the job cost ledger. This ledger contains the detailed records for every cost incurred by each construction project. The information in the job cost ledger has several uses, including the following:

- Compare accumulated costs to the budget, to see how well a project is doing in relation to the original bid
- Use the information as a historical basis for the preparation of new bids

To be effective, the ledger must store information at several levels. At a minimum, costs are charged to a project number, a project phase, and a cost code. A project phase can designate a separate part of the project, such as for each structure of an office complex. The cost codes are used to designate the type of expenditure.

A company can create its own list of cost codes, perhaps derived from a work breakdown structure, as described in the preceding section. Or, it can use a standardized set of cost codes. For example, the Department of Energy (DOE) uses the cost codes listed in the following exhibit for its construction projects.

Sample Cost Codes – Department of Energy

Code	Description	Code	Description
400	**Land and land rights**	5505	Wood and plastic
4010	Land	5506	Thermal and moisture protection
4020	Land rights	5507	Special construction
4030	Minerals	5508	Mechanical
4040	Timber	5509	Electrical
460	**Improvements to land**	**600**	**Utilities**
4601	Site preparation	6100	Communications systems
4602	Drainage	6150	Electrical transmission systems
4603	Landscaping	6210	Alarm systems
4605	Railroads	6250	Gas transmission systems
4606	Port facilities	6300	Irrigation systems
4700	Roads, walks and paved areas	6400	Sewerage systems
4800	Fences and guard towers	6450	Steam generation systems
4900	Other improvements to land	6500	Water supply & treatment systems
501	**Buildings**	6600	Oil piping and distribution
5011	Excavation and backfill	6900	Other utilities
5012	Concrete	**700**	**Special equipment/process systems**
5013	Masonry	7010	Vessels
5014	Metals	7020	Heat transfer
5015	Wood and plastic	7030	Mechanical equipment
5016	Finishes	7040	Package units
5017	Special construction	7050	Process piping
5018	Mechanical	7060	Electrical
5019	Electrical	7065	Instrumentation
550	**Other structures**	7070	Protective cover
5501	Excavation and backfill	7080	Reactor components
5502	Concrete	**800**	**Improvements for others**
5503	Masonry	**810**	**Demolition**
5504	Metals	**820**	**Tunneling**

Note: The preceding cost code list is not complete.

The preceding cost code list is clearly designed for commercial construction projects and is slanted toward the specific needs of the DOE (few construction companies have a need for the reactor components cost code!). Consequently, these cost codes would require a certain amount of conversion to one's specific needs.

The cost codes used for home building are quite different from those needed for commercial construction. The National Association of Home Builders has assembled the cost codes that appear in the following exhibit. This is a much more comprehensive list of cost codes than appeared in the preceding DOE list; it is not necessary to actually use every code on the list – instead, extract from it just those codes that are needed to separately accumulate the costs that are most relevant to a specific construction project. One way to do so is to create an account code in the job cost ledger only if there are funds budgeted for that classification of activity.

Sample Cost Codes – National Association of Home Builders

Code	Description	Code	Description
	PREPARATION & PRELIMINARIES	3120	Materials – wall framing
1000	**Permits and fees**	3130	Materials – roof framing
1010	Building permits	3140	Materials – trusses
1020	HBA assessments	3150	Materials – basement framing
1030	Warranty fees	3160	Framing labor
1100	**Architectural and engineering**	**3400**	**Concrete**
1110	Blueprints	3410	Concrete formwork
1120	Surveys	3420	Structural slabs
1200	**Site work**	3430	Structural frame
1210	Lot clearing	3440	Concrete stairs
1220	Fill dirt and material	3450	Precast decks and walls
1230	Rough grading	3460	Garage or carport slab
1300	**Demolition**	3470	Concrete labor
1400	**Utility connections**	**3500**	**Rough sheet metal**
1410	Temporary electric	3510	Gutters and downspouts
1420	Individual wells	3520	Metal edge and flashing
1430	Water service	3530	Soffit and gable flashing
1440	Septic systems	**3600**	**Rough plumbing**
1450	Sewer service	3610	Rough plumbing
1460	Gas service	3620	Rough plumbing labor
1470	Electric service	**3700**	**Rough electrical**
1480	Telephone service	3710	Rough electrical material
1490	Other utility connections	3720	Rough electrical labor
	EXCAVATION & FOUNDATION	**3800**	**Rough HVAC**
2000	**Excavation**	3810	Rough HVAC material
2010	Shoring	3820	Rough HVAC labor
2020	Earth hauling		FULL ENCLOSURE
2100	**Footing and foundations**	4000	Roofing
2120	Concrete blocks	4010	Roofing material
2130	Gravel	4020	Roofing labor
2140	Sand	**4100**	**Masonry**
2150	Rebar and reinforced steel	4110	Chimney
2160	Other foundation material	4120	Fireplace
2170	Labor footings and foundation	4130	Brick veneer
2200	**Waterproofing**	4140	Brick or stone wall
2300	**Termite protection**	4150	Masonry flooring
	ROUGH STRUCTURE	**4500**	**Windows and doors**
3000	**Steel**	4510	Windows
3010	Stairs – steel	4520	Skylights
3020	Beams – steel	4530	Storm windows and doors
3030	Posts – steel	4540	Exterior doors
3100	**Framing**	4550	Interior closet doors
3110	Materials – floor framing	4560	Sliding glass doors

Sample Cost Codes – National Association of Home Builders (continued)

Code	Description	Code	Description
4570	Garage doors	5410	Kitchen cabinets
4580	Window and door hardware	5420	Countertops
4590	Window and door installation	5430	Bathroom cabinets
4700	**Insulation**	5440	Cabinet hardware
4710	Foundation & basement insulation	**5500**	**Appliances**
4720	Roof and ceiling insulation	5510	Range
4730	Wall insulation	5520	Range hood
4740	Floor insulation	5530	Disposal
4750	Weather stripping and vapor barrier	5540	Dishwasher
4760	Insulation labor	5550	Refrigerator
4800	**Exterior trim**	5560	Washer dryer
4810	Posts and columns	5570	Microwave
4820	Siding	5580	Vacuum
4830	Shutters	5590	Others
4840	Cornices and rake trim	**5600**	**Finish plumbing**
4850	Exterior trim hardware	5610	Finish plumbing material
4860	Exterior trim labor	5620	Finish plumbing labor
4900	**Exterior painting**	**5700**	**Finish electrical**
4910	Exterior painting material	5710	Finish electrical material
4920	Exterior painting labor	5720	Finish electrical labor
	FINISHING TRADES	**5800**	**Finish HVAC**
5000	**Drywall**	5810	Finish HVAC material
5010	Drywall material	5820	Finish HVAC labor
5020	Drywall labor	**5900**	**Interior decoration**
5030	Drywall hanging	5910	Interior painting material
5040	Drywall finishing	5920	Interior painting labor
5100	**Flooring**	5930	Wall coverings
5110	Resilient flooring		COMPLETION AND INSPECTION
5120	Resilient floor installation	**6000**	**Building clean-up**
5130	Carpeting	6010	Building clean-up
5140	Carpet installation	**6100**	**Landscaping**
5150	Hardwood flooring	6110	Fill dirt
5160	Hardwood flooring install	6120	Top soil
5200	**Interior trim**	6130	Trees
5210	Moulding	6140	Shrubs
5220	Paneling	6150	Sod
5230	Closet shelving	6160	Seed
5240	Hardware – interior trim	6170	Fertilizer
5250	Interior trim labor	6180	Irrigation system
5300	**Ceramic tile**	**6200**	**Driveway**
5310	Ceramic trim	6210	Driveway materials
5320	Ceramic tile installation	6220	Driveway labor
5400	**Cabinets**	**6300**	**Exterior structures**

Sample Cost Codes – National Association of Home Builders (continued)

Code	Description	Code	Description
6310	Patio materials	6350	Fences – materials
6320	Patio labor	6360	Fences – labor
6330	Sidewalks – material	6370	Pads – materials
6340	Sidewalks – labor	6380	Pads – labor

Note: The preceding cost code list is not complete – it only states cost codes for direct construction. The cost codes for product definition, land development, financing, and indirect construction are not listed.

The cost codes used by the accounting department should be the same ones used by the estimating staff, so that the budget layout used by the estimators can be readily compared to the cost reports generated by the accounting staff.

A one-letter cost type code may be added to the end of each cost code. This additional code identifies a cost code as belonging to one of the main cost of construction classifications appearing within the income statement. These classifications are:

- Materials
- Labor
- Subcontractors
- Equipment
- Other

For example, the complete code for drywall labor (referencing the immediately preceding exhibit) would be 5020L, where the "L" denotes the labor classification. If this cost type code is included, the accounting system's report writer can then use it to aggregate and report on costs by these major classifications.

We have now discussed each component of an account code that would appear in the job cost ledger. Here is an example of what an entire account code might look like:

520-10-3020M

The breakdown of this account code is:

520 = Job number (unique identifier for the job)
10 = Phase (notes the phase of the work, such as apartment block #2)
3020M = Cost code (accumulates costs for steel beams, which are classified as materials)

A larger construction project may require the use of well over a hundred accounts (possible several thousand) in the job cost ledger. Given the potential size of these account listings, it makes sense to standardize their usage as much as possible. This means that everyone in the company, including accountants, buyers, and estimators, all use the same codes. In addition, the same coding structure should be used for long periods of time, so that the results of prior projects can be easily compared to current projects.

> **Tip:** Publish a standard list of job account codes, along with a definition of each code and an explanation of why it is used. This list should be issued to all employees who are in a position to need it, and should be re-issued whenever there are updates to the list.

One issue to watch for when creating job account codes is the tendency to have too many codes or to make them overly complex. When this happens, it is more difficult to assign costs to the correct codes, resulting in large variances in the budget versus actual reports because actual results are coded incorrectly. Consider the following options for simplifying job account codes and the manner in which costs are charged to them:

- Initially create the job codes with room for expansion. This means leaving space between the account numbers so that more accounts can be added in the future. Also, begin with enough digits for job codes and phase codes to accommodate large numbers of jobs and phases.
- Only allow changes to the existing codes when approved by senior management.
- Assign a default account code to each subcontractor, so that the accounting system automatically assigns their invoices to a specific code.
- Avoid splitting supplier invoices into multiple cost codes where possible.
- Create a standard cost code template that is loaded into the job cost ledger whenever a new job is created.
- If certain accounts are not expected to be used for a specific job, flag them in the accounting software as being blocked for that job.

Once job account codes have been loaded into the accounting system, also load in the budgeted costs for each of these codes. By doing so, the reporting system built into the software can then create budget versus actual reports for each account.

Job Cost Ledger Posting

Once information has been recorded in the job cost ledger, it is periodically summarized and posted to accounts in the general ledger, which in turn is used to construct the financial statements of the company. The account in the general ledger where this summarized information is stored is called a *control account*. The control accounts most likely to be associated with the job cost ledger are as follows:

- Cost of construction – materials
- Cost of construction – labor
- Cost of construction – subcontractors
- Cost of construction – equipment
- Cost of construction – other

For each of these control accounts, the cost stored in it for a reporting period should equal the aggregate amount of the accounts in the job cost ledger for the same reporting period that have the same cost type code. For example, the "cost of construction – materials" account balance for a specific reporting period should equal the sum of every account in the job cost ledger that has an "M" cost type code attached to it for that same reporting period.

If there is a difference between the information in the job cost ledger for a reporting period and the general ledger for the same reporting period, there are two possible reasons for it, which are:

- Not all of the information in the job cost ledger has been posted to the general ledger
- Someone has used a journal entry to record transactions directly into one or more of the control accounts

The accountant should investigate and correct any of these issues that may arise.

The Equipment Ledger

A construction company may have a significant investment in various types of construction equipment, such as backhoes, bulldozers, cranes and loaders. This equipment is expensive and incurs significant operating costs, so there should be a means for tracking equipment costs and billings, to establish whether it is worthwhile to have these investments. This tracking mechanism is the equipment ledger.

The equipment ledger is a subsidiary ledger that feeds into the general ledger (as was the case with the job cost ledger). The equipment ledger stores accounting information for each piece of equipment. The usual account structure within this ledger is to begin with a unique identification number for each piece of equipment and then track a variety of cost types for each piece of equipment. For example, a backhoe is assigned asset number 1200, while a bulldozer is assigned asset number 1205. This results in an account code structure within the equipment ledger that appears in the following exhibit. In the exhibit, the account code for each of the expenses matches the numbering that we used earlier in a sample chart of accounts.

Sample Equipment Ledger Account Code Structure

Account Code	Description
1200	**Backhoe**
1200-708	Backhoe – depreciation
1200-712	Backhoe – fuel and lubricant
1200-728	Backhoe – repairs and maintenance
1200-732	Backhoe – taxes and licenses
1205	**Bulldozer**
1205-708	Bulldozer – depreciation
1205-712	Bulldozer – fuel and lubricant
1205-728	Bulldozer – repairs and maintenance
1205-732	Bulldozer – taxes, licenses and insurance

An additional level of detail can be added below the account codes noted in the preceding exhibit, if actionable information can be obtained by doing so. For example, the taxes and licenses account could be subdivided to separately store costs for personal property taxes and operator's licenses.

As was the case with the job cost ledger, the information in the equipment ledger is periodically summarized and posted to control accounts in the general ledger. As a result of this posting process, the information in the equipment ledger for a reporting period should match the information in the control accounts in the general ledger for the same reporting period.

Summary

The account code structure for a construction company needs to be quite detailed, so that revenues and expenses can be separately reported for each individual job. Only then will managers be able to discern the ongoing performance of each open job and take action as necessary. A job cost ledger will be needed to track the costs of individual jobs, and perhaps also an equipment ledger. These two subsidiary-level ledgers are not usually found outside of the construction industry, which means that a construction-specific accounting software package will likely be required for any firm operating in the industry.

Chapter 3
Construction-Specific Accounting

Introduction

The bulk of the accounting transactions that a construction business deals with on a day-to-day basis are similar to those found in any other industry – payables, billings, cash collections, and payroll. However, there are some unique aspects to construction accounting that call for different treatment. In this chapter, we discuss the central issue of the timing to be used for recognizing revenues and costs, with a focus on the percentage of completion and completed contract methods. We also note a number of lesser construction issues, such as the handling of unpriced change orders, equipment cost allocations, and contract claims.

Accounting Standard-Setting Organizations

Where do the accounting rules come from? They are called accounting standards, and they are created by two organizations. One is the Financial Accounting Standards Board (FASB), which has created a massive set of accounting standards for entities operating within the United States. Actually, the FASB is the latest in a series of organizations that have been creating and refining accounting standards for many decades. A construction company operating within the United States will likely need to create financial statements that comply with the accounting standards issued by the FASB. The entire set of these standards, taken as a whole, is referred to as Generally Accepted Accounting Principles, or GAAP.

The other organization that creates accounting standards is the International Accounting Standards Board (IASB). The IASB has constructed the International Financial Reporting Standards, or IFRS. Most of the world other than the United States complies with IFRS. If a business is located outside of the United States or is owned by a foreign entity, it is likely that the entity's financial statements will be constructed using IFRS.

There are only a few major differences between GAAP and IFRS, though there are numerous smaller differences. The organizations have been working to reduce these differences for a number of years. It does not appear that the FASB and IASB will ever completely settle their differences, so it seems likely that there will be two different sets of accounting standards for the foreseeable future.

Lenders, creditors, and investors want construction companies to closely follow either GAAP or IFRS, so that they can more easily compare the financial statements of many organizations. When everyone follows the same rules when conducting their accounting, their financial statements should be quite comparable. For example, this means that a lender could compare the results of a construction company to those of a peer group to see how it is performing against a baseline. This comparison then tells the lender whether it should loan funds to the firm.

Types of Accounting Methodologies

A construction company can use one of two possible methodologies for its accounting, which are outlined in the following subsections. An accounting methodology is a set of rules used to determine when and how to report income and expenses.

Cash Method of Accounting

The cash method of accounting is used by many smaller businesses and is not confined to the construction industry. Instead, it is one of the more broadly applicable accounting methodologies. In essence, the cash method involves recognizing revenue when cash is received and recording expenses when expenditures are paid out. The difference between cash receipts and cash payments is profits (or losses).

The cash method is not considered to be theoretically correct, because the timing of cash receipts and cash payments can be manipulated. For example, a client pays an advance for a construction project, so the recipient records the cash as revenue – even though the project has not yet commenced. Similarly, if the payables manager decides to delay making a payment to a subcontractor, this means the company does not recognize the expense until the payment is made. In both cases, the reported income of the company is distorted. Despite being theoretically unsound, the cash method is allowed for smaller businesses, since it is the easiest way to keep the books and the Internal Revenue Service (IRS) allows it to be used for income tax returns. There is an IRS limitation on the use of the cash method for tax reporting, which is discussed in the Construction Tax Issues chapter.

Larger construction firms do not use the cash method, because outside auditors will refuse to provide an opinion on their financial statements if they use it. And, since lenders usually require audited financial statements before they will grant a loan, this keeps many construction firms from using the cash method.

Accrual Method of Accounting

The accrual method of accounting is used by larger businesses and is prevalent throughout industry. It is the accepted method under both GAAP and IFRS. In essence, the accrual method involves recognizing revenue when it is earned and expenses when consumed. Thus, there is no direct relationship between cash flows and the accrual method.

Under the accrual method, revenue is typically recognized when the client is billed. However, the amount of the retention is not recognized until the end of the project, because that is when the company has the right to receive it. Expenses are most commonly recognized when an invoice is received from a supplier or subcontractor. If the underlying goods or services have been received by the end of a reporting period but there is no corresponding invoice, then the company uses an accrual transaction to record the expense anyways (as covered in the Construction Transactions chapter).

A business will probably recognize both revenues and expenses earlier under the accrual method than under the cash method, since there is no delay while waiting for the transfer of cash. This can result in the reporting of more profits in the current year, which can accelerate the payment of income taxes that might have been delayed to a later year if the cash method had been used. This can be a problem when the cash payments associated with that revenue have not yet appeared, since the company must pay income taxes when it may not have enough cash to do so.

There are two variations on the accrual method that can be used for construction contracts, which are the percentage of completion method and the completed contract method. We deal with these two variations next.

Percentage of Completion Method

The percentage of completion method involves, as the name implies, the ongoing recognition of revenue and income related to longer-term projects. By doing so, the company can recognize some gain or loss related to a project in every accounting period in which the project continues to be active. For example, if a project is 20% complete, the company can recognize 20% of the expected revenue, expense, and profit.

The method works best when it is reasonably possible to estimate the stages of project completion on an ongoing basis, or at least to estimate the remaining costs to complete a project.

Conversely, this method should not be used when there are significant uncertainties about the percentage of completion or the remaining costs to be incurred. The estimating abilities of the business should be considered sufficient to use the percentage of completion method if it can estimate the minimum total revenue and maximum total cost with sufficient confidence to justify a contract bid.

The ability to create dependable contract estimates may be impaired when there are conditions present that are not normally encountered in the estimating process. Examples of these conditions are when a contract does not appear to be enforceable, there is litigation, or when related properties may be condemned or expropriated. In these situations, use the completed contract method instead (see the next subsection).

In essence, the percentage of completion method allows you to recognize as income that percentage of total income that matches the percentage of completion of a project. The percentage of completion may be measured in any of the following ways:

- *Cost-to-cost method.* This is a comparison of the contract cost incurred to date to the total expected contract cost. The cost of items already purchased for a contract but which have not yet been installed should not be included in the determination of the percentage of completion of a project, unless they were specifically produced for the contract. Also, allocate the cost of equipment over the contract period, rather than up-front, unless title to the equipment is being transferred to the customer.

- *Efforts-expended method.* This is the proportion of effort expended to date in comparison to the total effort expected to be expended for the contract. For example, the percentage of completion might be based on labor hours expended to date.
- *Units of work performed method.* This is the proportion of physical units of production that have been completed to date. For example, the percentage of completion could be based on material quantities installed, such as square yards of concrete laid or cubic yards of material excavated to date. This approach does not work well when significant costs are incurred prior to or following the production of physical units. For example, laying a pipeline involves building an access road to the pipeline location; the cost of con-structing the road would result in no earned revenues if the percentage of completion is based on the number of feet of pipe laid.

When it is difficult to derive the estimated cost to complete a contract, the recognition of profit is based on the lowest probable profit until the profit can be estimated with more accuracy. In cases where it is impractical to estimate any profit, other than to be assured that a loss will not be incurred, a zero profit is assumed for revenue recognition purposes; this means that revenues and expenses should be recognized in equal amounts until such time as more accurate estimates can be made. This approach is better than the completed contract method, since there is at least some indication of economic activity that spills over into the income statement prior to project completion.

The steps needed for the percentage of completion method are as follows:

1. Subtract total estimated contract costs from total estimated contract revenues to arrive at the total estimated gross margin.
2. Measure the extent of progress toward completion, using one of the methods just described.
3. Multiply total estimated contract revenue by the estimated completion percentage to arrive at the total amount of revenue that can be recog-nized.
4. Subtract the contract revenue recognized to date through the preceding period from the total amount of revenue that can be recognized. Recog-nize the result in the current accounting period.
5. Calculate the cost of earned revenue in the same manner. This means multiplying the same percentage of completion by the total estimated contract cost and subtracting the amount of cost already recognized to arrive at the cost of earned revenue to be recognized in the current ac-counting period.

This method is subject to fraudulent activity, usually involving the over-estimation of the amount of revenue and profit that should be recognized. Detailed documentation of project milestones and completion status can mitigate the possibility of fraud, but cannot eliminate it.

EXAMPLE

Logger Construction Company is building a maintenance facility on a military base. Logger has thus far accumulated $4,000,000 of costs related to the project and billed the client $4,500,000. The estimated gross margin on the project is 20%. Therefore, the total of expenses and estimated gross profit for the project is:

$$\$4,000,000 \text{ Expenses} \div (1 - 0.20 \text{ Gross margin}) = \$5,000,000$$

Since this figure is higher than the to-date billings of $4,500,000, Logger can recognize additional revenue of $500,000, using the following journal entry:

	Debit	Credit
Unbilled contract receivables	500,000	
Contract revenue earned		500,000

Logger should also recognize a proportional amount of expense to offset the amount of revenue recognized, for which the calculation is:

$$\$500,000 \text{ Additional contract revenue} \times (1 - 0.20 \text{ Gross margin}) = \$400,000$$

A key difference between the accrual method and the percentage of completion is that the percentage of completion method allows for the recognition of a portion of the retention over the course of a project. Thus, revenue recognition under the percentage of completion method is more aggressive than the accrual method. Nonetheless, the percentage of completion gives the most realistic view of the current financial results and financial position of a construction company.

Completed Contract Method

The completed contract method can be used when a business enters into a long-term contract (such as for the construction of property). This method is used to recognize all of the revenue and profit associated with a project only after the project has been completed. This method is used when there is uncertainty about the collection of funds due from a client under the terms of a contract. For example, it would be used for a speculative project where there is no buyer of a property.

This method yields the same results as the percentage of completion method, but only after a project has been completed. Prior to completion, this method does not yield any useful information for the reader of a company's financial statements. Also, since revenue and expense recognition only occurs at the end of a project, the timing of revenue recognition can be both delayed and highly irregular. Given these issues, the method should only be used under the following circumstances:

- When it is not possible to derive dependable estimates about the percentage of completion of a project; or
- When there are inherent hazards that may interfere with completion of a project; or
- When contracts are of such a short-term nature that the results reported under the completed contract method and the percentage of completion method would not vary materially.

If a contract is being accounted for under this method, record billings issued and costs incurred on the balance sheet during all periods prior to the completion of the contract and then shift the entire amount of these billings and costs to the income statement upon completion of the underlying contract. A contract is assumed to be complete when the remaining costs and risks are insignificant.

If there is an expectation of a loss on a contract, record it at once even under the completed contract method; do not wait under the end of the contract period to do so.

EXAMPLE

Logger Construction Company is building housing for a disaster relief agency and is doing so at great speed, so that displaced citizens can move in as soon as possible. Logger's management expects that the entire facility will be complete in just two months. Given the short duration of the project, Logger elects to use the completed contract method. Accordingly, Logger compiles $650,000 of costs on its balance sheet over the period of the project and then bills the client for the entire $700,000 fee associated with the project, recognizes the $650,000 of expenses, and recognizes a $50,000 profit.

When a contractor is using the completed contract method and there are unpriced change orders, the costs associated with those change orders should be deferred along with all other contract costs. However, if it does not appear that these incremental costs will be reimbursed, they should be charged to expense as incurred.

Summary of Accounting Methodologies

From a practical perspective, a smaller construction company should use the cash method, since it is the easiest way to conduct the accounting. Conversely, it should avoid the percentage of completion method, which requires the most accounting expertise to track. However, there is a cap on the size of a company that can use the cash method, so be prepared to switch methods once the company grows past a certain point.

If a contractor plans to use a surety firm for its bonding needs, be aware that the surety firm will likely require that the contractor prepare its financial statements using the percentage of completion method, which results in the most relevant information.

Unpriced Change Orders

A construction company is dealing with an unpriced change order when the parties cannot initially agree on the price to be charged by the company to the client for a modification of the underlying construction contract. The recovery of funds from an unpriced change order is considered probable when the following conditions are present:

- The client has approved of the scope change in writing; and
- The contractor has documented the related costs of the change; and
- The contractor has a favorable history of settling change orders.

There are three variations on how to deal with an unpriced change order. They are:

- When it is not probable that the costs associated with an unpriced change order will be paid back to the contractor through a price increase, the costs are added to the total estimated cost of the project; the result is a decline in the estimated amount of profit that the job will generate.
- When it is probable that an upward adjustment to the contract price will be forthcoming, defer the recognition of any costs incurred under the change order until the price has been settled.
- When it is probable that the prospective upward adjustment to the contract price will exceed the costs associated with the contract and the amount of the price can be reliably estimated, adjust the contract price to reflect the amount of the increase in costs. Do not recognize revenue exceeding the amount of costs incurred for the change order unless receipt of the estimated revenue amount is assured beyond a reasonable doubt.

When a change order is in dispute, it should be evaluated as a claim rather than a change order (see the next section).

Contract Claims

A construction company is not usually allowed to recognize any revenue associated with claims, given the risk that the client will not pay for them. Revenue recognition is only allowed when it is probable that additional revenue will result and that the amount of the additional revenue can be reliably estimated. For these criteria to be present, the following conditions must be satisfied:

- The evidence upon which the claim is based is objective and verifiable
- There is a legal basis for the claim or a legal opinion states that there is a legal basis for the claim
- The additional costs were caused by unforeseen circumstances
- The additional costs are not the result of the contractor's poor performance
- The costs linked to the claim are readily identifiable
- The costs linked to the claim are reasonable, based on the contractor's work

Even when all of the preceding conditions have been satisfied, the amount of revenue that can be recorded is limited to the contract costs associated with the claim.

Contract Back Charges

Back charges are billings for work performed by or paid for by one party that should have been handled by a different party. A high proportion of back charges are disputed by the recipient, which makes their collection less likely. When there is no dispute, a back charge can be billed to the recipient, with the amount of the charge being used to offset contract costs. However, when the back charge is in dispute, it is treated as a claim. See the preceding Contract Claims section for more information.

Costs Assigned to Jobs

There are several types of costs that may be assigned to a job. The ultimate goal of the accounting system is to accurately assign these costs to the correct jobs, so the accountant must have a clear understanding of which costs go where.

The first and most obvious cost classification is *direct costs*, which are those costs that will only be incurred if a job exists. Conversely, if the job does not exist, then these costs will not be incurred. Direct costs are comprised of materials, construction labor, and subcontractor costs. It is possible to charge the cost of small tools and equipment to a job as direct costs, especially when these items were acquired specifically for that job.

Tip: When small tools and equipment are charged to a specific job, they may still have some use after the job is over. Consequently, the theoretically correct approach is to then credit the job for the estimated salvage value of these items. This is not usually done in practice, because the estimated salvage value is immaterial.

There are also *indirect costs*. These costs do not go into the actual construction of a project, but are still needed to ensure that the project is completed on time and within budget. These costs include the following:

Contract supervision	Quality control
Depreciation	Repairs and maintenance
Indirect labor	Supplies
Inspection	Support costs
Insurance	Tools and equipment

Indirect costs should be allocated to jobs in a systematic and rational manner that can be easily replicated. Examples of such an allocation method are to charge indirect costs based on the cost of direct labor or the number of direct labor hours.

The direct cost percentage of total costs is quite high in the construction industry. In many other industries, the direct cost percentage is far lower, with indirect costs frequently exceeding direct costs.

When a cost cannot be clearly associated with a construction project, it is considered a period cost. A *period cost* is most closely associated with the passage of time. For example, the rent expense for the corporate headquarters office space is a period cost, because it is linked to a specific period of time. Most office wages and salaries are also considered to be period costs. Selling costs are treated as period costs.

Pre-contract costs are those costs incurred prior to the initiation of a contract. There are several rules for how these costs are to be accounted for, which are:

- When a pre-contract cost has been incurred for a specific contract that has not yet been finalized and the cost will not benefit the company unless the contract *is* finalized, the cost should be charged to expense as incurred.
- Assume the same scenario as was just described, except that recovery of the pre-contract costs is probable. In this case, the costs can be included in contract costs or inventory, which may result in deferred recognition.
- When pre-contract costs have been incurred to acquire or produce goods in anticipation of future contracts and cost recovery from the future contracts is probable, record the costs as inventory.
- When there are learning or start-up costs associated with existing contracts, even if these costs are in anticipation of follow-up projects, they should be charged to existing contracts.

There may be cases in which pre-contract costs are charged to expense as incurred, because the receipt of a contract is not considered probable. If the company then wins this contract, reversing the pre-contract expense is not allowed.

Labor Burden

Labor burden is the rate at which indirect labor costs are charged to each hour of labor. From an accounting perspective, this rate is used to charge indirect labor costs to a job. In addition, it is used to compile the total labor cost when developing a project bid. The sources of labor burden will depend on the benefits offered by the individual company. These sources may include many of the following costs:

- Employer matching portion of payroll taxes
- Employer-paid payroll taxes
- Dental insurance
- Disability insurance
- Health club fees
- Life insurance
- Medical insurance
- Pension contributions
- Unemployment insurance

- Workers' compensation insurance

Labor burden is added to an employee's wages to arrive at the total cost of labor for that individual. The burden rate is the dollar amount of burden (i.e., overhead) that is applied to one dollar of wages. For example, if the annual benefits and payroll taxes associated with an individual is $20,000 and his wages are $80,000, then the burden rate is $0.25 per $1.00 of wages.

Equipment Cost Allocation

There can be many costs associated with the use and ongoing maintenance of construction equipment. Some of these costs are rental fees, lubrication, replacement tires, gasoline, depreciation, and periodic servicing. These costs are typically accumulated by piece of equipment and then allocated to individual jobs. The allocation is needed because each piece of equipment may be used on a number of projects in order to increase its utilization.

It is not acceptable to charge one job for the cost of a major equipment replacement just because the replacement occurred on the day when the equipment was being used on that specific job site. Realistically, the replacement was needed because of many hours of prior utilization that was spread across several jobs. Consequently, a more appropriate accounting treatment is to allocate equipment costs based on the projected usage of each piece of equipment by each job to which it is assigned.

What is the cost assignment methodology when a construction company is in possession of construction equipment for a long period of time, rather than simply renting it for a single job? In this situation, it is likely that there are ongoing maintenance and financing costs associated with the equipment every month, even though the usage level of the equipment may vary. This situation is set forth in the following example.

EXAMPLE

Hodgson Construction owns a backhoe loader. Hodgson charges $400 of depreciation to expense in each month and pays $200 of insurance as part of the ongoing fixed costs of owning the backhoe – even if the equipment is not used.

During the winter months of November through March, the backhoe is not used, but Hodgson still incurs $600 of costs in each of these months. The company actively uses the backhoe from April through October of each year; during this time, additional costs related to maintenance, lubrication and fuel sum to $4,000 per month. Thus, the costs incurred by Hodgson for the backhoe, by month, are as follows:

41

Month	Fixed Costs	Variable Costs	Total Costs
January	$600		$600
February	600		600
March	600		600
April	600	$4,000	4,600
May	600	4,000	4,600
June	600	4,000	4,600
July	600	4,000	4,600
August	600	4,000	4,600
September	600	4,000	4,600
October	600	4,000	4,600
November	600		600
December	600		600
Totals	$7,200	$28,000	$35,200

To refer back to the preceding example, the company could simply charge its equipment costs to expense during the periods when there are no jobs. However, doing so means that the company is absorbing a portion of the total annual cost of the equipment, thereby undercharging its jobs. A better approach is to charge the entire annual cost of the equipment to jobs. This concept is explained in the following example.

EXAMPLE

We continue with the preceding example concerning the cost of Hodgson Construction's backhoe loader. In a typical year, Hodgson's owner estimates that the backhoe will be actively used on jobs for 700 hours. By dividing the total annual cost of $35,200 by the 700 estimated usage hours, he arrives at a cost per billable hour of $50.29.

The owner wants to ensure that all equipment costs incurred during the year are billed to jobs, so that the company does not absorb any equipment costs. To do so, he decides to bill each job at the predetermined $50.29 rate. However, the backhoe is only used from April to October, which has an unusual effect on how the equipment expense appears in the company's income statement. From January to March and from November to December, the company will still absorb the full amount of the expense. From April to October, there will be a negative expense, because the rate at which the cost is being charged covers the entire annual cost of the backhoe. This effect appears in the following table, showing the actual results experienced by Hodgson:

Month	Actual Costs Incurred	Actual Hours Billed	Billing Rate/Hour	Total Billed	Cumulative Charge
January	$598	0	$50.29	$0	$598
February	595	0	50.29	0	1,193
March	602	0	50.29	0	1,795
April	4,550	85	50.29	4,275	2,070
May	5,088	110	50.29	5,532	1,626
June	5,041	112	50.29	5,632	1,035
July	4,420	98	50.29	4,928	527
August	4,270	92	50.29	4,627	170
September	5,942	132	50.29	6,638	-526
October	3,167	64	50.29	3,219	-578
November	610	10	50.29	503	-471
December	612	0	50.20	0	141
Totals	$35,495	703		$35,354	

The table shows that Hodgson absorbs some equipment cost during the first few months of the year, after which the amounts billed to projects offset this expense, to the point where the expense is even negative from September through November. By the end of the year, slight differences between the budgeted and actual costs and billed hours result in Hodgson absorbing $141 of equipment cost.

The largest part of the equipment expense can be repairs and maintenance, especially when tires, engines, or other major parts must be replaced. These expenditures can cause a significant spike in the costs incurred for equipment. These items should be lumped in with the other equipment expenses for billing to projects, as noted in the preceding two examples. One should attempt to predict the amount of larger one-time expenditures and include them in the formulation of the hourly charge that will be billed to jobs. Otherwise, the amount billed to jobs will not reflect the total amount of equipment expense incurred.

Summary

Though it is more complex to formulate, the percentage of completion method is likely to be the method of choice when recognizing construction revenues and costs, since it does the best job of providing information about profits occurring over the course of a project. The accounting for unpriced change orders, claims, and back charges is significantly more conservative, where there needs to be clear proof of a forthcoming payment before any revenue can be recognized. This latter accounting is justified, since any billings departing from the base-level contract may have a significantly reduced probability of being paid.

Chapter 4
Construction Transactions

Introduction

The accountant needs to be aware of the most common transactions that must be recorded in the accounting records of a construction company. An accounting transaction is a business event having a monetary impact on the financial statements and is recorded in the accounting records. Examples of accounting transactions are:

- Sale to a client
- Receive cash in payment of an invoice owed by a client
- Purchase fixed assets from a supplier
- Record the depreciation of a fixed asset over time
- Purchase job materials from a supplier
- Invest in marketable securities
- Borrow funds from a lender
- Issue a dividend to investors
- Sale of assets to a third party

In this chapter, we begin with a discussion of how transactions are recorded, using double entry accounting and journal entries. We then proceed into a review of how various transactions are recorded in the accounting records.

Double Entry Accounting

Double entry accounting is a record keeping system under which every transaction is recorded in at least two accounts. There is no upper limit on the number of accounts used in a transaction, but the minimum is two accounts. There are two columns in each account, with debit entries on the left and credit entries on the right. In double entry accounting, the total of all debit entries must match the total of all credit entries. When this happens, a transaction is said to be *in balance*. If the totals do not agree, the transaction is *out of balance*. An out of balance transaction must be corrected before financial statements can be created.

The definitions of a debit and credit are:

- A debit is an accounting entry that either increases an asset or expense account, or decreases a liability or equity account. It is positioned to the left in an accounting entry.
- A credit is an accounting entry that either increases a liability or equity account, or decreases an asset or expense account. It is positioned to the right in an accounting entry.

An account is a separate, detailed record associated with a specific asset, liability, equity, revenue, expense, gain, or loss. Examples of accounts and their characteristics are noted in the following table.

Characteristics of Sample Accounts

Account Name	Account Type	Normal Account Balance
Cash	Asset	Debit
Accounts receivable - trade	Asset	Debit
Inventory	Asset	Debit
Fixed assets	Asset	Debit
Accounts payable	Liability	Credit
Accrued expenses	Liability	Credit
Notes payable	Liability	Credit
Capital stock	Equity	Credit
Retained earnings	Equity	Credit
Revenue	Revenue	Credit
Cost of construction	Expense	Debit
Depreciation	Expense	Debit
Office rent	Expense	Debit
Salaries and wages	Expense	Debit
Gain on sale of asset	Gain	Credit
Loss on sale of asset	Loss	Debit

The key point with double entry accounting is that a single transaction always triggers a recordation in *at least* two accounts, as assets and liabilities gradually flow through a business and are converted into revenues, expenses, gains and losses.

Journal Entries

A journal entry is a formalized method for recording a business transaction. It is recorded in the accounting records of a business, usually in the general ledger, but sometimes in a subsidiary ledger that is then summarized and rolled forward into the general ledger.

Journal entries are used in a double entry accounting system, where the intent is to record every business transaction in at least two places. For example, when a company pays an employee, this reduces the cash (asset) account while increasing the salaries and wages (expense) account.

The structure of a journal entry is:

- A header line may include a journal entry number and entry date.

- The first column includes the account number and account name into which the entry is recorded. This field is indented if it is for the account being credited.
- The second column contains the debit amount to be entered.
- The third column contains the credit amount to be entered.
- A footer line may also include a brief description of the reason for the entry.

Thus, the basic journal entry format is:

	Debit	Credit
Account name / number	$xx,xxx	
Account name / number		$xx,xxx

The structural rules of a journal entry are that there must be a minimum of two line items in the entry and that the total amount entered in the debit column equals the total amount entered in the credit column.

A journal entry is usually printed and stored in a binder of accounting transactions, with backup materials attached that justify the entry. This information may be accessed by the company's auditors as part of their annual auditing activities.

There are several types of journal entries, including the following:

- *Adjusting entry*. An adjusting entry is used at month-end to alter the financial statements to bring them into compliance with the relevant accounting framework (such as GAAP or IFRS). For example, a company could accrue unpaid wages at month-end in order to recognize the wages expense in the current period.
- *Compound entry*. This is a journal entry that includes more than two lines of entries. It is frequently used to record complex transactions or several transactions at once. For example, the journal entry to record a payroll usually contains many lines, since it involves the recordation of numerous tax liabilities and payroll deductions.
- *Reversing entry*. This is an adjusting entry that is reversed as of the beginning of the following period, usually because an expense was accrued in the preceding period and is no longer needed. For example, a wage accrual in the preceding period is reversed in the next period, to be replaced by an actual payroll expenditure.

In general, journal entries are not used to record high-volume transactions, such as client billings or supplier invoices. These transactions are handled through specialized software modules that present a standard on-line form to be filled out. Once the form is complete, the software automatically creates the accounting record.

General Entries

We begin with a sampling of the accounting transactions that apply to the general operations of a construction company, such as rent payments, paying suppliers, and receiving cash from clients. In each of the following sub-sections, we describe the transaction and how it is set up in a journal entry.

Office Rent Expense

There are many types of general expenses incurred by a construction company that are not directly related to jobs. Instead, these expenses are required to keep the entire organization operational. An example is office rent, which is paid when the company is occupying space under a lease agreement. When recording office rent, the charge is made to the office rent account, with an offsetting increase in the accounts payable – trade account.

EXAMPLE

Alibaba Construction receives an $18,000 rent invoice from its landlord for the current month. This invoice results in an $18,000 increase in the company's expenses and an increase in its liabilities. The journal entry is:

	Debit	Credit
Office rent	18,000	
Accounts payable - trade		18,000

It is quite possible that the company will receive the landlord's rent invoice prior to the month to which the invoice relates. When this invoice is received early, the invoice is recorded as a prepaid expense, which is a current asset account. With the passage of time, the invoice will eventually relate to the current month, at which point the invoice amount is shifted out of the prepaid expense account and is charged to expense.

EXAMPLE

Alibaba Construction receives an $18,000 invoice for its May office rent. On the receipt date, it is late April. The accountant records the invoice with the following entry:

	Debit	Credit
Prepaid expenses	18,000	
Accounts payable - trade		18,000

At the beginning of May, the accountant records the following entry to charge the invoice to expense:

	Debit	Credit
Office rent	18,000	
Prepaid expenses		18,000

A lease agreement with a landlord may state that there will be escalations in the amount of rent to be paid over the term of the lease. For example, the cost may be $25.00 per square foot in the current year, which increases to $25.25 throughout the next year and then increases again to $25.50 in the third year. The accounting for this arrangement is called *straight-line rent*, where the total liability under the lease is charged to expense on an even periodic basis over the term of the lease.

To calculate straight-line rent, aggregate the total cost of all lease payments and divide by the total lease term. The result is the amount to be charged to expense in each month of the lease. This calculation should include all discounts from the normal rent, as well as extra charges that can reasonably be expected to be incurred over the life of the lease.

The calculation of straight-line rent may result in a monthly rent expense that differs from the actual amount billed by the landlord. This is usually because the landlord has built escalating lease payments into the lease agreement. In such a case, the straight-line amount charged to expense is higher than the actual amount billed during the first part of the lease, and lower than the amount billed during the last part of the lease.

This initial disparity, where the amount of the expense is greater than the amount paid, is charged to an accrued liability account. The latter disparity, where the amount paid is greater than the amount of the expense, is a reversal of the accrued liability account. By the end of the lease, the accrued liability account will have a zero balance.

EXAMPLE

The Sunrise Construction Company enters into a short-term facility lease where the amount billed is $500 per month for the first six months and $600 per month for the last six months. On a straight-line basis, the amount of rent is $550 per month. In the first month of the lease, Sunrise records the following entry:

	Debit	Credit
Office rent	550	
Cash		500
Accrued expenses		50

In the last month of the lease, Sunrise records the following entry:

	Debit	Credit
Office rent	550	
Accrued expenses	50	
Cash		600

Other General Expenses

The journal entry logic just used for the recordation of office rent applies to most other general expenses that a construction company may incur. In essence, when an invoiced amount applies to the current period, it is charged immediately to expense. If the invoiced amount arrives in advance of the period to which it applies, the amount is initially recorded as a prepaid expense, which is an asset, and then recognized as an expense in the period to which it applies. In addition, it is possible that the company will not receive an invoice in the month to which it applies. If so, and the accountant wants to ensure that the expense is recorded in the correct period, it is possible to accrue the expense. In an accrual situation, the accountant creates a journal entry for an expense and an offsetting accrued liability. This journal entry results in the recognition of the appropriate expense in the correct period. In addition, the entry automatically reverses in the next reporting period, resulting in a negative expense. The actual invoice is then recorded when it is received in the next reporting period, which offsets the negative expense, resulting in the recognition of no expense in the next period. The concept of an expense accrual is addressed in the following example.

EXAMPLE

Horton Contractors normally receives a monthly invoice for $800 from the local cell phone provider. In June, the invoice does not arrive, so Horton's accountant elects to accrue the expense. She does so with the following entry:

	Debit	Credit
Telephone expense	800	
Accrued expenses		800

This entry results in the recognition of an $800 telephone expense in June. As soon as the books are closed for June and opened for July, the accounting system automatically reverses the transaction with the following journal entry:

Construction Transactions

	Debit	Credit
Accrued expenses	800	
Telephone expense		800

The reversal eliminates the accrued expenses liability from the books. Thus far, there is $800 of telephone expense in June and -$800 of telephone expense in July. The supplier's invoice then arrives in July and is entered into the accounting system. This results in the recognition of $800 of telephone expense in July and an account payable liability. The $800 expense exactly offsets the -$800 expense already recognized in July. In summary, the net result of these transactions has been the recognition of the telephone expense in June, while there is now a valid obligation to pay the supplier.

Accrual transactions will result in more accurate financial statements, but require some additional time to close the books at the end of each accounting period. Consequently, it is customary to only use accruals when the amount of the expense is relatively large. Below a certain threshold level, it is not considered efficient to create journal entries for small amounts that will not have a material effect on the financial statements.

Inventory Purchases

A company may acquire materials before it has a specific use for them. If so, these purchases are designated as inventory, rather than being charged to a specific job. When such a purchase is made, the inventory asset account is increased, as is the relevant accounts payable account. There is no initial impact on the income statement, since the inventory has not yet been consumed.

EXAMPLE

The purchasing manager for Arduous Construction buys extra lumber in order to take advantage of favorable prices. The price is $26,000. When the supplier's invoice is recorded in the accounting system, the resulting journal entry is:

	Debit	Credit
Inventory	26,000	
Accounts payable – trade		26,000

Supplier Invoice Payments

The payment of an invoice may occur many weeks after it was received from a supplier or subcontractor. The payment of an invoice is an entirely separate transaction from its original recordation. When a payment is made, the cash account declines by the amount of the payment, while the amount in the relevant accounts payable account is removed. This results in equal reductions from the asset and liability sides of the balance sheet.

EXAMPLE

Adelaide Construction pays a $4,000 invoice for steel beams. This action results in the balance in the cash account declining by $4,000, while the accounts payable – trade account also declines by $4,000. The journal entry is:

	Debit	Credit
Accounts payable – trade	4,000	
Cash		4,000

An invoice payment rarely requires the accountant to prepare a manual journal entry. Instead, the accounts payable module of the accounting software automatically prepares the entry. All the accountant has to do is indicate which invoices are to be paid and to load check stock into a computer printer.

Client Cash Receipts

When a client pays the company, the impact is only on the company's balance sheet. The amount of the payment reduces the related account receivable, while increasing the firm's cash balance.

EXAMPLE

Elder Construction receives a check for $50,000 from a client, which pays for an invoice that Elder's accountant had previously mailed to the client. This payment is for a non-retention billing. The resulting journal entry is:

	Debit	Credit
Cash	50,000	
Accounts receivable - trade		50,000

As was the case with the creation of an invoice to a client, the accountant does not need to create a journal entry. Instead, the accountant accesses the cash receipts module in the accounting system, flags the invoice being paid, enters the amount of the payment, and the system automatically creates the journal entry.

A construction company may offer its clients an early payment discount, especially if it is in immediate need of cash. If so, the client will pay a reduced amount, perhaps 1% or 2% less than the face amount of an invoice. When an invoice is paid in this manner, the full amount of the invoice must still be removed from the accounting records, so a sales discounts account is used to record the amount of the early payment discount.

EXAMPLE

In the preceding example involving Elder Construction, the company had instead offered the client a 1% discount if it paid the invoice within 10 days of receipt. The client accepts this offer and pays Elder $49,500. The journal entry to record this transaction is:

	Debit	Credit
Cash	49,500	
Sales discounts	500	
Accounts receivable - trade		50,000

The sales discounts account is a contra revenue account, which means that it offsets and therefore reduces the amount of revenue that the organization can recognize.

Loan Acquisition

A construction firm may need to obtain a short-term loan to cover its working capital needs. If so, the entry is an increase in the cash account and an increase in the notes payable account. These changes only impact the balance sheet.

EXAMPLE

Finnegan Construction obtains a $100,000 working capital loan, to be repaid within one year. Finnegan's accountant records the loan with the following entry.

	Debit	Credit
Cash	100,000	
Notes payable		100,000

The notes payable entry was not made to the long-term notes payable account, since the loan should be repaid within one year.

An alternative way to obtain a loan is to acquire a fixed asset on long-term credit. In effect, the company is being given equipment or some other asset in exchange for assuming a loan liability – there is no receipt of cash by the company. It is possible that the company will make a down payment on a portion of the asset cost, which reduces the amount of the loan.

EXAMPLE

Seagull Construction acquires a road grader for $70,000. The grader is purchased on credit, with Seagull making a $10,000 down payment and taking on a three-year loan for the remaining $60,000 cost of the equipment. Seagull's accountant records the transaction with the following journal entry:

	Debit	Credit
Fixed assets – construction equipment	70,000	
Long-term notes payable		60,000
Cash		10,000

Loan Payments

The accountant can use the information on an amortization schedule (which appears in the Debt Accounting chapter) to create the journal entries needed to record loan payments. For example, the journal entry needed to record a loan payment that includes a loan pay down of $8,523 and an interest charge of $4,000 is:

	Debit	Credit
Long-term notes payable	8,523	
Interest expense	4,000	
Cash		12,523

Sale of Stock

A contractor may be incorporated, in which case it can sell shares of stock to investors. When there is a sale, the amount received is recorded in the common stock account as a credit, with the cash from the sale being recorded as a debit to the cash account. The basic journal entry format is:

	Debit	Credit
Cash [asset account]	x,xxx	
Common stock [equity account]		x,xxx

A complication arises if the company is required to state a par value on its stock certificates. Par value was originally intended to be a minimum amount below which an entity's dividends could not drop the amount of stockholders' equity, and was originally designed to represent a reserve for creditors. The par value is typically stated at such a minor amount (such as $0.01), however, that it affords no significant protection to creditors. In some states, there is no requirement to have par value at all. When there is a par value requirement, the amount paid to the company by an investor must be split between the common stock account (which contains the par value) and the additional paid-in capital account, which contains the rest of the payment. For example, a company sells 1,000 shares for $10 each, where the par value is $0.01 per share. The resulting journal entry is:

	Debit	Credit
Cash [asset account]	10,000	
Common stock [equity account]		10
Additional paid-in capital [equity account]		9,990

Entries Related to the Percentage of Completion

When a company uses the percentage of completion method to recognize the outcome of jobs, there are two possible entries that might be required. One is to record changes in costs and profits in excess of the amount billed thus far to the client. The basic journal entry format is:

	Debit	Credit
Costs and profits in excess of billings [asset account]	x,xxx	
Unbilled revenues [revenue account]		x,xxx

The amount recorded each month for costs and profits in excess of billings is the net change between the underbillings in the preceding month and the current month. This entry will increase profits and creates an asset on the balance sheet.

It is also possible that the company has billed clients more than its costs and profits. If so, the accountant must record as a liability the excess amount of the billings. This entry also reduces the amount of recognized revenue. The basic journal entry format is:

	Debit	Credit
Excess billings [revenue account]	x,xxx	
Billings in excess of costs and profits [liability account]		x,xxx

The amount recorded each month for billings in excess of costs and profits is the net change between the overbillings in the preceding month and the current month. This entry will reduce profits and creates a liability on the balance sheet.

When there are several jobs open, it is possible that the company will have costs and profits in excess of earnings on some jobs, and billings in excess of costs and profits on other jobs. These amounts cannot be combined into a single line item on the balance sheet. Instead, they must be kept separate, so that the aggregate amount of costs and profits in excess of earnings is stated as an asset and the aggregate amount of billings in excess of costs and profits is stated as a liability.

Anticipated Losses on Contracts

The accountant must record a loss whenever the costs to be incurred for a contract will be greater than the revenues earned from it. The amount of the loss is the difference between these two figures and must be recognized in full as soon as the loss becomes evident. This situation arises when a company is using either the percentage of completion method or the completed contract method.

When a loss is anticipated, the accountant creates a provision for a loss. A sample journal entry is:

	Debit	Credit
Loss on contract [loss account]	x,xxx	
Loss reserve on existing contracts [see following note]		x,xxx

There are two ways in which the loss reserve can be classified on the balance sheet. It may be stated separately as a current liability, or it may appear on the asset side of the balance sheet as an offset to the costs that have been accumulated for a project.

Job Costing Entries

In the following sub-sections, we cover a number of entries that can be recorded in the job cost ledger.

Invoice Charged to Job

A construction company may receive any number of invoices from suppliers and subcontractors that relate to a job. When one of these invoices is recorded in the accounting system, it has the following effects:

- *Impact on balance sheet*. When the company has delayed payment terms with a supplier or subcontractor, the invoice is classified as an account payable. This is a liability that appears in the current liabilities section of the balance sheet. If the company instead pays cash up-front, then there is no accounts payable liability. Instead, the cash account (an asset) declines by the amount of the payment. No matter what the method of payment may be, there is an additional change to the retained earnings line item, which is discussed shortly.
- *Impact on job cost ledger*. The expenditure is recorded in the job cost ledger. The amount is charged to a specific job number, phase, cost code, and cost type code, as described earlier in the Construction Accounting System chapter.
- *Impact on income statement*. The information in the job cost ledger is periodically posted to the general ledger, from which the income statement is derived. When posted, the invoice is charged to one of the construction expense accounts – materials, labor, subcontractors, equipment, or other. Doing so reduces the profits of the business. When profits change, this

amount is reflected in the retained earnings line item within the equity section of the balance sheet. Thus, adding an expense to the income statement reduces the retained earnings balance in the balance sheet.

EXAMPLE

Hodgson Construction receives a $4,000 invoice for steel beams related to Phase 10 of its job number 520. The cost code for steel beams is 3020. The cost type code is "M," since the invoice is for construction materials. The effects are:

- Increase in $4,000 of the accounts payable – trade account
- Charge of $4,000 to job code 502-10-3020M in the job cost ledger
- When the ledger posts to the general ledger, $4,000 is charged to the cost of construction – materials account
- Following the posting to the general ledger, the retained earnings balance is automatically reduced by $4,000

There may be cases in which a construction company withholds a retention amount from a supplier or subcontractor invoice, to be paid at a later date. This introduces one change in the entry, which is that the amount of the retention is recorded in the accounts payable – retention account rather than the accounts payable – trade account. The concept is expanded upon in the following example, where a retention amount is withheld from the invoice of a subcontractor.

EXAMPLE

Eskimo Construction receives a $2,500 invoice for exterior painting labor from a subcontractor. This relates to Phase 2 of its job number 315. The cost code for exterior painting labor is 4920. The cost code type is "S," since the invoice is from a subcontractor. Eskimo is withholding 20% of the invoice as a retention amount. The effects are:

- Increase in $2,000 of the accounts payable – trade account
- Increase in $500 of the accounts payable – retention account
- Charge of $2,500 to job code 315-02-4920S in the job cost ledger
- When the ledger posts to the general ledger, $2,500 is charged to the cost of construction – subcontractors account
- Following the posting to the general ledger, the retained earnings balance is automatically reduced by $2,500

There are not many instances in which a retention amount is withheld from a materials invoice, since suppliers will not stand for this type of payment delay. Instead, retentions are normally withheld against subcontractor invoices to provide an incentive for subcontractors to perform.

It is quite possible that an incoming invoice contains a multitude of line items, each containing a separate charge. If so, the invoice is charged to as many job codes as necessary to account for every item on the invoice.

Labor Charged to a Job

The calculation and classification of labor costs is a significant topic, so we have included it in the Payroll Accounting chapter.

Inventory Charged to a Job

When inventory is charged to a specific job, the inventory asset account declines by the amount of the charge, which is stored in the job cost ledger. When this ledger is posted to the general ledger, the charge appears in the cost of construction – materials account.

When charging the cost of inventory items to specific jobs, a possible concern is what to do when there are several of the items in inventory, and they were purchased at different costs. There are three possibilities for how to determine the cost to charge a job, which are:

- Charge the weighted-average cost of the inventory items.
- Assume that the earlier units added to stock are the ones being used first (known as first in, first out), so use the cost of the oldest units.
- Assume that the latest units added to stock are the ones being used first (known as last in, first out), so use the cost of the newest units.

The method used should be applied consistently over time. A possible issue is that the last in, first out method is not allowed under international financial reporting standards, so if the company plans to issue its financial statements outside of the United States, it should consider using a different approach to charging inventory costs to jobs. For more information about these variations in costing, see the author's *Accounting for Inventory* book.

Client Billings

A construction company may issue a series of invoices to a client, depending on the duration of the job and the contract terms. Whenever an invoice is issued, the essential journal entry is a debit to an account receivable account and a credit to a revenue account. This entry results in an increase in the accounts receivable asset on the balance sheet and an increase in the revenues (and therefore profits) reported on the income statement.

A variation on the basic billing entry occurs when there is a retention arrangement in the contract with a client. In this case, the accountant may split the billed amount into an amount that is payable now and an amount that is payable at the end of the job. In this case, the journal entry expands somewhat to include a line item for the accounts receivable – retention account.

EXAMPLE

Zillow Construction has reached a milestone in its construction project for a key client. The agreement with the client allows Zillow to bill the client $1,000,000, of which $100,000 is designated as retention, to be paid at a later date. The accountant prepares the following journal entry to record the billing:

	Debit	Credit
Accounts receivable - trade	900,000	
Accounts receivable - retention	100,000	
Revenue		1,000,000

The accountant does not usually prepare a journal entry for a billing. Instead, the invoice is prepared through the billing module in the company's accounting software. Once completed, the software automatically prepares the journal entry.

When a client billing is prepared, the amount of the revenue may be posted to the job cost ledger, rather than the general ledger. The revenue amount is then posted to the general ledger whenever the information in the job cost ledger is summarized and posted to the general ledger. By recording the initial transaction in the job cost ledger, a complete record of all revenues is stored within that ledger. However, the accountant may elect to only store job *costs* in the job cost ledger, and so chooses to instead record the revenue transaction directly into the general ledger.

Equipment Entries

In the following sub-sections, we cover a number of entries that can be recorded in the equipment ledger.

Equipment Rentals

When a construction company rarely uses a certain type of construction equipment, it is more likely to rent the equipment only for the period when it will be needed for a construction task. In this case, the rental charge is recorded in the equipment ledger, with the offsetting liability charged to the accounts payable – trade account. The ledger balance will eventually be posted to the general ledger, where the equipment rental charge will appear in the cost of construction – equipment account.

Equipment Repairs

When the accountant receives a supplier invoice for equipment repairs, this amount is logged into the accounting system as an account payable, with the expense charged to the specific equipment item in the equipment ledger. When the ledger balance is posted to the general ledger, the repair cost will appear in the cost of construction – equipment account.

Other costs related to equipment, such as fuel and periodic maintenance costs, are charged to the equipment ledger in the same manner as equipment repairs.

Equipment Charged to a Job

A construction company can incur substantial costs to rent or own the equipment used on its construction sites, so these costs should be charged to jobs. Doing so allows for more accurate billings and results in a clear picture of the profitability of individual jobs.

Equipment costs are allocated to jobs based on the amount of time they are used on each job. This calls for an equipment timesheet that is quite similar to an employee timesheet. The equipment timesheet is used to record the time worked on various jobs, phases, and cost codes. The time recorded in this manner is then multiplied by a standard hourly rate to arrive at an equipment charge, which is recorded in the job cost ledger. Alternatively, the amount of the actual equipment cost can be determined precisely and then allocated to the various jobs that used the equipment.

EXAMPLE

Chrysanthemum Construction has leased a backhoe for a construction project at a lease cost of $12,400. The company has also incurred fuel costs of $580 and repair costs of $1,020. These costs were all charged to the equipment ledger, resulting in a total backhoe cost of $14,000.

The project managers have been maintaining equipment timesheets for the backhoe while the company has been using it. The timesheets are compiled into the following table, showing an hours-based allocation of the equipment costs to the various jobs:

Project	Hours Charged Against	Percentage of Total Time	Cost Allocation
A	140	14%	$1,960
B	360	36%	5,040
C	420	42%	5,880
D	80	8%	1,120
Totals	1,000	100%	$14,000

The amount of the equipment allocation can be recorded in the equipment ledger, which reduces the expense recorded in the ledger.

Summary

A construction company may deal with a massive number of accounting transactions, especially when it is managing a large number of jobs over the course of a year. If transactions are not charged to the correct accounts every time, it is quite likely that job-level profits will be reported incorrectly – and the errors may be substantial. Consequently, it is helpful to adopt a regimented approach to the entry of construction transactions in the accounting records, which means:

- The use of standard procedures for recording transactions
- Training new accounting staff based on these procedures
- Using pre-constructed journal entry templates, so that the same accounts are used every time

It can take a long time to arrive at an accounting system that is free of transactional errors. A good way to achieve this goal is to dig into every error found in order to locate and correct the reason for the error. The eventual outcome will be carefully controlled accounting processes that work right, every time.

Chapter 5
Construction Financial Statements

Introduction

Once a business has accumulated accounting information for a period of time, the information is aggregated into financial statements. There are three key financial statements, which are the balance sheet, income statement, and statement of cash flows. These documents are used to evaluate the financial position, results and cash flows of an organization, respectively. The statements are most heavily used by the management team of the business, which employs them as a feedback loop that reveals the results of their activities during the past reporting period. In addition, financial statements are examined by surety firms that are contemplating assisting the company with its bonding needs, as well as by lenders and creditors, to see if the firm can pay back its obligations.

In this chapter, we explore the layout and content of each of the financial statements, along with the disclosures that should accompany a complete set of statements.

The Balance Sheet

The balance sheet reveals the assets, liabilities, and equity of a construction firm as of a specific date, which is stated in the header of the report. It is typically prepared at the end of each reporting period, such as once a month, quarter, or year. We present a sample balance sheet in the following exhibit. The layout in the exhibit includes every asset, liability, and equity account listed in the chart of accounts that was presented in the preceding chapter.

Sample Balance Sheet

Herringbone Construction Company
Balance Sheet
as of 12/31/20X1

ASSETS		LIABILITIES	
Cash	$70,000	Accounts payable - trade	$140,000
Accounts receivable - trade	300,000	Accounts payable - retention	$9,000
Accounts receivable - retention	28,000	Billings in excess of costs and profits	13,000
Allowance for doubtful accounts	-11,000	Notes payable	50,000
Marketable securities	45,000	Accrued expenses	18,000
Inventory	5,000	Warranty reserves	20,000
Costs and profits in excess of billings	27,000	Other current liabilities	25,000
Notes receivable	12,000	TOTAL CURRENT LIABILITIES	$275,000
Prepaid expenses	8,000		
Other current assets	11,000	Long-term notes payable	325,000
TOTAL CURRENT ASSETS	$495,000	TOTAL LIABILITIES	$600,000
FIXED AND OTHER ASSETS		OWNER'S EQUITY	
Fixed assets - buildings	430,000	Capital stock	10,000
Fixed assets – construction equipment	70,000	Additional paid-in capital	190,000
Fixed assets – office equipment	20,000	Retained earnings	200,000
Fixed assets – vehicles	40,000	TOTAL EQUITY	$400,000
Accumulated depreciation	-65,000		
Other assets	10,000		
TOTAL ASSETS	$1,000,000	TOTAL LIABILITIES & EQUITY	$1,000,000

In the balance sheet, the total of all assets equals the sum of all liabilities and equity, which is known as the *accounting equation*. Thus, the accounting equation is:

$$Assets = Liabilities + Equity$$

If there are a large number of accounts in the chart of accounts, this can result in an excessively large balance sheet that is difficult to read. To keep the presentation of the report manageable, some of the accounts may be merged together into a single line item. For example, the two accounts receivable accounts appearing in the preceding exhibit could be combined into a single "accounts receivable" line item, while the four fixed asset accounts could be merged into a single "fixed assets" line item.

There are several sub-totals listed in the balance sheet. These are the subtotal for current assets and the subtotal for current liabilities. These subtotals are required by the accounting standards, so that a user can compare the two figures and estimate whether a construction firm has sufficient liquid assets to pay for its more immediate liabilities.

The Income Statement

The income statement contains the results of the operations of a business during a reporting period, showing revenues and expenses and the resulting profit or loss. This report covers all activities occurring within the period, usually spanning a month, quarter, or year.

The income statement is compiled from accounts listed in the chart of accounts, which are usually those listed in the chart after the accounts used to create the balance sheet. The statement begins with revenues and then subtracts expenses to arrive at a profit or loss. We present a sample income statement in the following exhibit that includes every revenue and expense account listed in the chart of accounts from the preceding chapter.

Sample Income Statement

Granny Construction Company
Income Statement
for the month ended December 31, 20X2

Revenue	$3,000,000
Construction costs	
Materials	700,000
Labor	565,000
Subcontractors	1,400,000
Equipment	80,000
Other	5,000
Total construction costs	2,750,000
Gross profit	$250,000
Overhead costs	
Advertising and promotions	$2,000
Bank fees	1,000
Benefits	24,000
Charitable contributions	1,000
Depreciation	18,000
Dues and memberships	500
Fuel and lubrication	2,500
Insurance	4,500
Interest expense	5,000
Janitorial expenses	1,500
Office rent	21,000
Office supplies	1,500
Postage and delivery	500
Professional fees	5,500
Repairs and maintenance	12,500
Salaries and wages	68,000

Taxes and licenses	2,000
Telephones	3,500
Training	500
Travel and entertainment	2,500
Utilities	4,000
Warranty expense	10,000
Other income	-3,000
Other expenses	1,500
Profit before tax	$60,000
Income taxes	21,000
Net profit	$39,000

Many of the costs listed within the "overhead" classification on the preceding income statement can be traced to a specific job, though not to a specific task within that job. If so, these costs can still be justifiably allocated to a job. Examples of these allocable costs are:

- Job supervision labor
- Job trailer rental or depreciation
- Fuel, lubrication, repairs, maintenance, and depreciation on the equipment used on a project

There is a linkage between the information reported in the balance sheet and the income statement. When a profit or loss is reported in the income statement, it is added to the retained earnings line item in the equity section of the balance sheet. For example, a company has retained earnings of $50,000 at the beginning of January and earns $6,000 during that month. The $6,000 appears in the net profit figure on the income statement and is added to the retained earnings figure on the balance sheet, resulting in an ending retained earnings balance of $56,000.

The Statement of Cash Flows

The statement of cash flows contains information about the flows of cash into and out of a company; in particular, it shows the extent of those company activities that generate and use cash. It is particularly useful for assessing the differences between net income and the related cash receipts and payments.

The statement of cash flows does not replace the income statement. The income statement measures the revenues, expenses, and profit or loss generated during a reporting period. The cash flows that appear on the statement of cash flows do not necessarily match the income and loss information on the income statement, so both statements are needed to provide the most complete picture of the results generated by an entity.

In the statement of cash flows, cash flow information is to be reported within three separate classifications. The use of classifications is intended to improve the quality of the information presented. These classifications are:

- *Operating activities*. These are an entity's primary revenue-producing activities. Operating activities is the default classification, so if a cash flow does not belong in either of the following two classifications, it belongs in this classification. Operating cash flows are generally associated with revenues and expenses. Sample operating activities are segregated into cash inflows and outflows in the following table.

Sample Operating Activity Cash Inflows and Outflows

Cash Inflows	Cash Outflows
Cash receipts from the sale of goods and services	Cash payments to employees
Cash receipts from the collection of receivables	Cash payments to suppliers
Cash receipts from lawsuit settlements	Cash payment of fines
Cash receipts from settlement of insurance claims	Cash payments to settle lawsuits
Cash receipts from supplier refunds	Cash payments of taxes
Cash receipts from licensees	Cash refunds to customers
	Cash payment of interest to creditors
	Cash payment of contributions

- *Investing activities*. These are investments in productive assets, as well as in the debt and equity securities issued by other entities. These cash flows are generally associated with the purchase or sale of assets. Sample investing activities are segregated into cash inflows and outflows in the following table.

Sample Investing Activity Cash Inflows and Outflows

Cash Inflows	Cash Outflows
Cash receipts from the sale of equity investments	Cash payments made to acquire equity investments
Cash receipts from the collection of principal on a loan	Cash payments made to acquire debt securities
Cash receipts from the sale of fixed assets	Cash payments made to acquire fixed assets

- *Financing activities*. These are the activities resulting in alterations to the amount of contributed equity and an entity's borrowings. These cash flows are generally associated with liabilities or equity and involve transactions between the reporting entity and its providers of capital. Sample financing activities are segregated into cash inflows and outflows in the following table.

Sample Financing Activity Cash Inflows and Outflows

Cash Inflows	Cash Outflows
Cash receipts from the sale of company shares	Cash payments to pay dividends
Cash receipts from the issuance of debt instruments	Cash payments to buy back company shares
Cash receipts from a mortgage	Cash payments for debt issuance costs
Cash receipts from derivative instruments	Cash payments to pay down principal on debt

The order of presentation in the statement of cash flows is as just described – operating activities, followed by investing activities, and then financing activities.

Some types of cash flows could be classified as being in more than one of the preceding classifications. If so, the designated classification should be based on the activity most likely to provide the majority of cash flows for an item.

There are two methods for presenting the statement of cash flows, which are the direct method and the indirect method. The indirect method is by far the most popular, so that is the only one we are presenting. Under the indirect method, the presentation begins with the net income or loss experienced in the reporting period, with subsequent additions to or deductions from that amount for non-cash revenue and expense items, resulting in cash provided by operating activities. Adjustments to the net income figure that are needed to derive cash flows from operating activities include:

- Accrued revenue
- Accrued expenses, such as a provision for bad debt losses
- Noncash expenses, such as depreciation
- Gains and losses from the sale of assets
- Change in accounts receivable
- Change in inventory
- Change in accounts payable

The format of the indirect method appears in the following example. Note that the indirect method does not include actual cash inflows and outflows in the cash flows from operating activities section, but rather an approximate derivation of cash flows based on adjustments to net income.

Sample Statement of Cash Flows

Iago Construction Company
Income Statement
for the month ended December 31, 20X3

Cash flows from operating activities		
Net income		$3,000,000
Adjustments for:		
Depreciation	$125,000	
Provision for losses on accounts receivable	20,000	
Gain on sale of facility	-65,000	
		80,000
Increase in trade receivables	-250,000	
Decrease in costs and profits in excess of billings	325,000	
Decrease in trade payables	-50,000	
		25,000
Cash generated from operations		3,105,000
Cash flows from investing activities		
Purchase of fixed assets	-500,000	
Proceeds from sale of equipment	35,000	
Net cash used in investing activities		-465,000
Cash flows from financing activities		
Proceeds from issuance of common stock	150,000	
Proceeds from issuance of long-term debt	175,000	
Dividends paid	-45,000	
Net cash used in financing activities		280,000
Net increase in cash		2,920,000
Cash at beginning of period		2,080,000
Cash at end of period		$5,000,000

Financial Statement Disclosures

A number of disclosures may accompany the financial statements. These disclosures are intended to provide additional information about the financial situation of a business. These disclosures are required by the applicable accounting standards, and may result in dozens of pages of additional content for a large company. A smaller contractor may find that just a few disclosures will be sufficient for meeting the requirements of the accounting standards. In this section, we cover just those disclosures that are most likely to apply to the financial statements of a business in the construction industry. The disclosures are:

- *Backlog on existing contracts.* State the amount of backlog of uncompleted projects in comparison to the backlog from one year ago. It is encouraged, but not required, that contractors present backlog information for signed contracts where cancelation is not anticipated. A variation is to disclose a backlog schedule that shows the beginning backlog, new contract awards, revenue recognized from contracts, and the ending backlog. For example:

  > As of December 31, 20X2, the company had a backlog of $2.7 million of uncompleted projects where cancelation of the underlying contracts was not anticipated. In comparison, the company's backlog on December 31, 20X1 was $2.4 million.

- *Contract costs.* Note the aggregate amount within contract costs that relates to unapproved change orders, claims and similar items that are subject to uncertain outcomes. Also describe the principal items within this aggregate total and their status. Further, state the amount of any progress payments that have been netted against any contract costs in the balance sheet. For example:

  > As of December 31, 20X2, the company recorded $12,000 of capitalized contract costs that relates to unapproved change orders and claims. Of this amount, $10,000 relates to the Carbuncle account, for which we are confident that the full amount will be approved by the client within the next month.

- *Deferred costs.* Note the company's policy for deferring the recognition of any costs in anticipation of a future sale and state the amounts involved. For example:

  > The company always recognizes all costs incurred in anticipation of future sales in the period incurred.

- *Joint ventures.* If the company participates in joint ventures, disclose the methods used to report these joint ventures in its financial statements. For example:

  > The company is a 32% owner of the BioPly Construction Consortium. Given its ownership percentage, the company is considered to have significant influence over BioPly, and so uses the equity method to account for its ownership interest.

- *Operating cycle.* A contractor may have an operating cycle that significantly exceeds one year. If so, state that this is the case and the extent to which it alters the reporting of current assets and current liabilities (which are supposed to be liquidated within one operating cycle). For example:

Certain contracts that the company has with its clients have durations that can extend up to two years. The operating cycle for these contracts therefore extends for up to two years. We classify the assets and liabilities associated with these contracts as current assets and current liabilities, respectively.

- *Receivables – retainage.* Disclose the amounts of any receivables billed to customers under contract retainage agreements and which have not yet been paid. Also note the amounts expected to be collected within one year and the years in which any additional retainage will be collected. For example:

  Accounts receivable includes amounts due from clients of $234,000 at December 31, 20X1 that have been retained pending the completion of contracts and customer acceptance of deliverables. The full amount is expected to be collected within one year. Retentions are usually due 30 days following the completion of a project and acceptance by the customer.

- *Receivables - uncertain.* Disclose the amounts and status of any billed or unbilled amounts that are for claims, unapproved change orders and similar items where it is uncertain that payment will be received. For example:

  The company has included in its accounts receivable $32,000 of claims for which payment by clients is not certain.

- *Revenue recognition.* The construction industry uses unique revenue recognition methods, so disclose which ones are being used. If the percentage of completion method is used, describe how progress toward completion is being measured, such as by calculating labor hours to date or costs incurred to date. If the completed contract method is being used, justify why this is the case, such as by noting the presence of undependable estimates of completion. For example:

  The company uses the percentage of completion method in calculating its recognition of job revenue and costs. Progress toward completion is measured by comparing hours worked to-date to the total estimated number of hours for each job.

- *Use of estimates.* State any revisions in the estimates of job percentages of completion. This is only necessary if the revisions are material. For example:

  The company currently uses the percentage of completion method to recognize the revenue and costs associated with eight of its projects. Of these projects, we have altered the percentage of completion for the Hoosier Bridge project downward, from 45% on October 31 to 38% as of December 31, 20X3. The reason for the change was the discovery that the foundations for the bridge were eroding due to an improper concrete mix, which will require reconstruction of a portion of the foundations.

Reporting Options

The income statement represents the most aggregated way in which the profitability of a business can be reported. In a construction company, there are a number of ways to subdivide various parts of the business in order to obtain a more detailed analysis of where profits and losses originate. The accountant can assist in this analysis by providing a variety of reports. Here are several possibilities:

- *Customer-level reporting.* A company may work on multiple jobs for a specific customer. If so, it is useful to aggregate job profits for each customer, to see if working with certain customers results in unusually high or low profits. It is possible that this analysis could trigger the decision to avoid working with certain customers and to build closer relations with others.
- *Job-level reporting.* This is the most obvious reporting option, where the revenues and expenses associated with each individual job are stated in separate reports. This is generally an easy task, since the information in the job cost ledger can be used to generate the reports. A variation on the concept is to report by types of jobs (such as reporting separately for retail homes, apartments, and warehouses), to see if the company performs especially well or poorly on certain types of jobs.
- *Equipment-level reporting.* A potentially valuable reporting option is to track the revenues and costs associated with each piece of equipment owned by the company. This information can be extracted from the equipment ledger. The report may reveal that some equipment is being underutilized; if so, a reasonable option may be to sell the equipment and instead rent it for the short periods when it is actually needed. The analysis may also reveal whether any equipment is costing an excessive amount for maintenance and so should be replaced.
- *Crew-level reporting.* Measure the schedule performance index for each crew (see the Construction Analysis chapter), which (over time) will identify those crews that are consistently the most efficient or inefficient. In addition, the quality of their work can be reviewed and indicated within the same report. This information is useful for assigning the best crews to the most time-sensitive aspects of a job. The information needed for this report is not stored within the accounting system.
- *Estimator reporting.* The person who creates bids can be a significant driver of profitability, since a poorly-derived bid will either result in a lost sale or in an accepted sale that has little chance of earning a profit. Consequently, track all bids issued by the company and who was responsible for issuing each bid. Then report on bids won and lost by estimator, as well as the profitability of projects by estimator.

- *Subcontractor reporting.* Measure the schedule performance index for each subcontractor, as well as their ability to perform within the cost boundaries set by their contracts and the quality of their work.

Summary

The preparation of a complete set of financial statements and accompanying disclosures can be a formidable undertaking for the accountant. Luckily, it may be possible to issue a reduced set of statements during most months of the year. The management team typically only wants to see the balance sheet and income statement, so the statement of cash flows and disclosures are not issued. Only when an outside party wants to see the financial statements is it advisable to prepare a more comprehensive document. Disclosures are usually only added when the audited year-end financial statements are being prepared.

Chapter 6
Fixed Asset Accounting

Introduction

A construction company may have a substantial investment in construction equipment and may also own a significant amount of office and storage space. When this is the case, the accountant must create classifications for the assets, decide which expenditures should be recorded as assets, and depreciate them over time. This chapter delves into the types of asset classifications, the capitalization limit, the concept of base units, different types of depreciation, and other issues relating to the proper accounting for fixed assets.

Related Podcast Episode: Episode 139 of the Accounting Best Practices Podcast discusses a lean system for fixed assets accounting. It is available at: **accounting-tools.com/podcasts** or **iTunes**

What are Fixed Assets?

The vast majority of the expenditures that a construction company makes are related to jobs, such as for materials and labor. The effect of these items passes through the organization quickly – they are recorded within jobs and charged to expense over the course of those jobs, or no later than by the end of the jobs. Thus, the benefits they generate are short-lived.

Fixed assets are entirely different. These are items that generate economic benefits over a long period of time. Because of the long period of usefulness of a fixed asset, it is not justifiable to charge its entire cost to expense when incurred. Instead, the *matching principle* comes into play. Under the matching principle, a business should recognize both the benefits and expenses associated with a transaction (or, in this case, an asset) at the same time. To do so, we convert an expenditure into an asset and use depreciation to gradually charge it to expense.

By designating an expenditure as a fixed asset, we are shifting the expenditure away from the income statement, where expenditures normally go, and instead place it in the balance sheet. As we gradually reduce its recorded cost through depreciation, the expenditure flows from the balance sheet to the income statement. Thus, the main difference between a normal expenditure and a fixed asset is that the fixed asset is charged to expense over a longer period of time.

The process of identifying fixed assets, recording them as assets, and depreciating them is time-consuming, so it is customary to build some limitations into the process that will route most expenditures directly to expense. One such limitation is to charge an expenditure to expense immediately unless it has a useful life of at least one year. Another limitation is to only recognize an expenditure as a fixed asset if it exceeds a certain dollar amount, known as the *capitalization limit*. These limits keep the vast majority of expenditures from being classified as fixed assets, which reduces the work of the accountant.

EXAMPLE

Starburst Construction incurs expenditures for three items and the accountant must decide whether it should classify them as fixed assets. Starburst's capitalization limit is $2,500. The expenditures are:

- It buys a very used backhoe for $3,000. The accountant expects that the backhoe only has six months of useful life left, after which it should be scrapped. Since the useful life is so short, the accountant elects to charge the expenditure to expense immediately.
- It buys a laptop computer for $1,500, which has a useful life of three years. This expenditure is less than the capitalization limit, so it is charged to expense.
- It constructs a new construction storage shed for $200,000, which has a useful life of 20 years. Since this expenditure has a useful life of longer than one year and a cost greater than the capitalization limit, the accountant records it as a fixed asset and will depreciate it over its 20-year useful life.

An alternative treatment of the $3,000 backhoe in the preceding example would be to record it in the Other Assets account in the balance sheet and charge the cost to expense over six months. This is a reasonable alternative for expenditures that have useful lives of greater than one accounting period, but less than one year. It is a less time-consuming alternative for the accountant, who does not have to create a fixed asset record or engage in any depreciation calculations.

Fixed Asset Classifications

If an expenditure qualifies as a fixed asset, it must be recorded within an account classification. Account classifications are used to aggregate fixed assets into groups, so that the same depreciation methods and useful lives can be applied to them.

You also usually create general ledger accounts by classification and store fixed asset transactions within the classifications to which they belong. Here are the most common classifications used:

- *Buildings*. This account may include the cost of acquiring a building or the cost of constructing one. If the purchase price of a building includes the cost of land, apportion some of the cost to the Land account (which is not depreciated).
- *Computer equipment*. This classification can include a broad array of computer equipment, such as routers, servers, and backup power generators. It is useful to set the capitalization limit higher than the cost of desktop and laptop computers, so that an excessive number of these assets are not tracked.

- *Construction equipment.* This classification includes all types of equipment that may be used on job sites, and so may contain the largest invested amount of any fixed asset account.
- *Furniture and fixtures.* This is one of the broadest categories of fixed assets, since it can include many types of office furniture and room furnishings.
- *Intangible assets.* This is a non-physical asset, such as a permit to engage in construction activities.
- *Land.* This is the only asset that is not depreciated, because it is considered to have an indeterminate useful life. Include in this category all expenditures to prepare land for its intended purpose, such as demolishing an existing building or grading the land.
- *Land improvements.* Include in this account any expenditures that add functionality to a parcel of land, such as irrigation systems, fencing, and landscaping.
- *Leasehold improvements.* These are improvements to leased space that are made by the tenant and typically include office space, air conditioning, telephone wiring, and related permanent fixtures.
- *Office equipment.* This account contains such equipment as copiers, printers, and video equipment. Some companies elect to merge this classification into the furniture and fixtures classification, especially if they have few office equipment items.
- *Software.* This account includes larger types of departmental or company-wide software, such as job cost tracking software and purchasing software. Many desktop software packages are not sufficiently expensive to exceed the corporate capitalization limit and so will be charged directly to expense.
- *Vehicles.* This account contains automobiles, vans, and similar types of rolling stock.

Tip: Do not create too many sub-classifications of fixed assets, such as automobiles, vans, light trucks, and heavy trucks within the main "vehicles" classification. If the classification system is too finely divided, there will inevitably be some "crossover" assets that could fall into several classifications. Also, having a large number of classifications requires extra tracking work by the accountant.

EXAMPLE

The president of American Construction wants to be true to the company's name and become a national-caliber construction company. As part of this vision, he decides to construct a new company headquarters in an especially parched area of the Nevada desert. American purchases land for $3 million, updates the land with irrigation systems for $400,000 and constructs an office tower for $10 million. It then purchases furniture and fixtures for $300,000. The company aggregates these purchases into the following fixed asset classifications:

Expenditure Item	Classification	Useful Life	Depreciation Method
Building - $10 million	Building	30 years	Straight line
Furniture and fixtures - $300,000	Furniture and fixtures	7 years	Straight line
Irrigation - $400,000	Land improvements	15 years	Straight line
Land - $3 million	Land	Indeterminate	None

Tip: The local government that charges a company a personal property tax may require that the business complete its tax forms using certain asset classifications. It may make sense to contact the government to determine the classifications under which it wants the company to report, and adopt these classifications as the company's official classification system. By doing so, it will not be necessary to re-aggregate assets for personal property tax reporting.

Accounting for Fixed Assets

There are several key points in the life of a fixed asset that require recognition in the accounting records; these are the initial recordation of the asset, the recognition of depreciation, and the eventual derecognition of the asset. There may also be cases in which the value of an asset is impaired. We describe these general concepts in the following bullet points:

- *Initial recognition.* There are a number of factors to consider when initially recording a fixed asset, such as the base unit, which costs to include, and when to stop capitalizing costs.
- *Depreciation.* The cost of a fixed asset is gradually charged to expense over time, using depreciation. There are a variety of depreciation methods available, which are described in later sections.
- *Impairment.* There are numerous circumstances under which an asset's recorded value is considered to be impaired. If so, the value of the asset is written down on the books of the company.
- *Derecognition.* When an asset comes to the end of its useful life, the organization will likely sell or otherwise dispose of it. At this time, remove it from the accounting records, as well as record a gain or loss (if any) on the final disposal transaction.

The Capitalization Limit

One of the most important decisions to be made in the initial recognition of a fixed asset is what minimum cost level to use, below which an expenditure is recorded as an expense in the period incurred, rather than as a fixed asset. This capitalization limit, which is frequently abbreviated as the *cap limit*, is usually driven by the following factors:

- *Asset tracking.* If an expenditure is recorded as a fixed asset, the fixed asset tracking system may impose a significant amount of control over the newly-recorded fixed asset. This can be good, if you want to know where an asset is at any time. Conversely, there is not usually a tracking system in place for an expenditure that is charged to expense, since the assumption is that such items are consumed at once and so require no subsequent tracking.

- *Fixed asset volume.* The number of expenditures that will be recorded as fixed assets will increase dramatically as the cap limit is lowered. For example, there may only be one fixed asset if the cap limit is $100,000, 50 assets if the cap limit is $10,000, and 500 assets if the cap limit is $1,000. Analyze historical expenditures to estimate a cap limit that will prevent the accountant from being deluged with additional fixed asset records.

- *Profit pressure.* Senior management may have a strong interest in reporting the highest possible profit levels right now, which means that they want a very low cap limit that shifts as many expenditures as possible into capitalized assets. Since this pressure can result in a vast number of very low-cost fixed assets, this issue can create a considerable work load for the accountant.

- *Record keeping.* The accountant can spend a considerable amount of time tracking fixed assets, formulating depreciation and eliminating fixed assets from the records once they have been disposed of. This can be quite a burden if there are a large number of assets.

- *Tax requirements.* Some government entities require a business to report fixed assets, so that they can charge a personal property tax that is calculated from the reported fixed asset levels. Clearly, a high cap limit will reduce the number of reported fixed assets, and therefore the tax paid. However, government entities may require a minimum cap limit in order to protect their tax revenues.

From an efficiency or tax liability perspective, a high cap limit is always best, since it greatly reduces the work of the accountant and results in lower personal property taxes. From a profitability or asset tracking perspective, you would want the reverse, with a very low cap limit. These conflicting objectives call for some discussion within the management team about the most appropriate cap limit – it should not simply be imposed on the company by the accountant.

The Base Unit

There is no specific guidance in the accounting standards about the unit of measure for a fixed asset. This unit of measure, or *base unit*, is essentially a company's definition of what constitutes a fixed asset. This definition can be formalized into a policy, so that it is applied consistently over time. Here are several issues to consider when creating a definition of a base unit:

- *Aggregation.* Should individually insignificant items be aggregated into a fixed asset, such as a group of tables or chairs? This increases the administrative burden, but does delay recognition of the expense associated with the items.

> **Tip:** If the company is billed by a supplier for several assets on a single invoice, do not record everything on the invoice as a single fixed asset. Instead, determine the base unit for each asset and allocate the freight and tax for the entire invoice to the individual fixed assets that you choose to recognize.

- *Component replacement.* Is it likely that large components of an asset will be replaced during its useful life? If so, designate the smaller units as the most appropriate base unit to track in the accounting records. This decision may be influenced by the probability of these smaller components actually being replaced over time. For example, the roof of a building could be designated as a separate asset, since it may be replaced several times over the life of the building.
- *Identification.* Can you identify an asset that has been designated as a base unit, or at least attach an asset tag to it? If not, you will not be able to subsequently track it and so should not designate it as a base unit. This is a common problem in a larger business that may have dozens of identical tables, chairs, and other furniture.
- *Legal description.* If there is a legal description of an asset, such as is stated on a tax billing for a specific parcel of land, this can form the basis for a base unit, since you can then associate future expenses billed by a government entity to the base unit.
- *Tax treatment.* Is there a tax advantage in separately accounting for the components of a major asset? This may be the case where the useful life of a component is shorter than that of a major asset of which it is a part, so that it can be depreciated quicker.
- *Useful life.* The useful lives of the components of a base unit should be similar, so that the entire unit can be eliminated or replaced at approximately the same time.

EXAMPLE

Oklahoma Construction maintains office buildings in areas that are subject to major hailstorms, which commonly result in hail damage to the roofs of the buildings. On average, hail damage will require the replacement of a roof every ten years, while the rest of each structure is estimated to be viable for at least 50 years. Given these differences, it makes sense for the company to designate the roofs as separate base units.

The Initial Measurement of a Fixed Asset

Initially record a fixed asset at the historical cost of acquiring it, which includes the costs to bring it to the condition and location necessary for its intended use. These activities include the following:

- Physical construction of the asset
- Demolition of any preexisting structures
- Renovating a preexisting structure to alter it for use by the buyer
- Administrative and technical activities during preconstruction, such as designing the asset and obtaining permits
- Administrative and technical work after construction commences, such as litigation, labor disputes, and technical problems

EXAMPLE

A construction company decides to add an additional air conditioning unit to its main office, which involves the creation of a concrete pad for the unit, stringing electrical cabling to it, linking it to the building's air conditioning vents, and obtaining an electrical permit. All of the following costs can be included in the fixed asset cost of the unit:

Air conditioning unit price	$120,000
Concrete pad	3,000
Wiring and ducts	5,000
Electrical permit	200
Total	$128,200

The Purpose of Depreciation

The purpose of depreciation is to charge to expense a portion of an asset that relates to the revenue generated by that asset. This is called the matching principle, where revenues and expenses both appear in the income statement in the same reporting period, which gives the best view of how well a company has performed in a given accounting period. The trouble with this matching concept is that there is usually only a tenuous connection between the generation of revenue and a specific asset.

To get around this linkage problem, we usually assume a steady rate of depreciation over the useful life of each asset, so that we approximate a linkage between the recognition of revenues and expenses. This approximation threatens our credulity even more when a company uses accelerated depreciation, since the main reason for using it is to defer taxes (and not to better match revenues and expenses).

If we were not to use depreciation at all, we would be forced to charge all assets to expense as soon as we buy them. This would result in large losses in the months when this purchase transaction occurs, followed by unusually high profitability in those periods when the corresponding amount of revenue is recognized, with no offsetting expense. Thus, a company that does not use depreciation will have front-loaded expenses and extremely variable financial results.

Depreciation Concepts

There are three factors to consider in the calculation of depreciation, which are as follows:

- *Useful life*. This is the time period over which it is expected that an asset will be productive, or the amount of activity expected to be generated by it. Past its useful life, it is no longer cost-effective to continue operating the asset, so the company would dispose of it or stop using it. Depreciation is recognized over the useful life of an asset.

> **Tip:** Rather than recording a different useful life for every asset, it is easier to assign each asset to an asset class, where every asset in that asset class has the same useful life. This approach may not work for very high-cost assets, where a greater degree of precision may be needed.

- *Salvage value*. When a company eventually disposes of an asset, it may be able to sell the asset for some reduced amount, which is the salvage value. Depreciation is calculated based on the asset cost, less any estimated salvage value. If salvage value is expected to be quite small, it is generally ignored for the purpose of calculating depreciation.

EXAMPLE

Acorn Construction buys an employee shuttle van for $75,000 and estimates that its salvage value will be $15,000 in five years, when it plans to dispose of the asset. This means that Acorn will depreciate $60,000 of the asset cost over five years, leaving $15,000 of the cost remaining at the end of that time. Acorn's accountant expects to then sell the asset for $15,000, which will eliminate the asset from its accounting records.

- *Depreciation method*. Depreciation expense can be calculated using an accelerated depreciation method, or evenly over the useful life of the asset. The advantage of using an accelerated method is that a business can recognize more depreciation early in the life of a fixed asset, which defers some income tax expense recognition to a later period. The advantage of using a steady depreciation rate is the ease of calculation. Examples of accelerated depreciation methods are the double declining balance and sum-of-the-years' digits methods. The primary method for steady depreciation is the straight-line method.

The *mid-month convention* states that, no matter when a fixed asset is purchased in a month, it is assumed to have been purchased in the middle of the month for depreciation purposes. Thus, if a fixed asset was purchased on January 5th, assume that it was bought on January 15th; or, if it was acquired on January 28, still assume that it was bought on January 15th. By doing so, it is easier to calculate a standard half-month of depreciation for the first month of ownership.

If you choose to use the mid-month convention, this also means that you should record a half-month of depreciation for the *last* month of the asset's useful life. By doing so, the two half-month depreciation calculations equal one full month of depreciation.

Many companies prefer to use full-month depreciation in the first month of ownership, irrespective of the actual date of purchase within the month, so that they can slightly accelerate their recognition of depreciation, which in turn reduces their taxable income in the near term.

Accelerated Depreciation

Accelerated depreciation is the depreciation of fixed assets at a very fast rate early in their useful lives. The primary reason for using accelerated depreciation is to reduce the reported amount of taxable income over the first few years of an asset's life, so that a company pays a smaller amount of income taxes during those early years. Later on, when most of the depreciation will have already been recognized, the effect reverses, so there will be less depreciation available to shelter taxable income. The result is that a company pays more income taxes in later years. Thus, the net effect of accelerated depreciation is the deferral of income taxes to later time periods.

A secondary reason for using accelerated depreciation is that it may actually reflect the usage pattern of the underlying assets, where they experience heavy usage early in their useful lives.

There are several calculations available for accelerated depreciation, such as the double declining balance method and the sum of the years' digits method. We will describe these methods in the following sub-sections.

All of the depreciation methods end up recognizing the same amount of depreciation, which is the cost of the fixed asset less any expected salvage value. The only difference between the various methods is the speed with which depreciation is recognized.

Accelerated depreciation requires additional depreciation calculations and record keeping, so some companies avoid it for that reason (though fixed asset software can readily overcome this issue). They may also ignore it if they are not consistently earning taxable income, which takes away the primary reason for using it. Companies may also ignore accelerated depreciation if they have a relatively small amount of fixed assets, so that the tax effect of using accelerated depreciation is minimal.

Sum-of-the-Years' Digits Method

The sum of the years' digits (SYD) method is used to calculate depreciation on an accelerated basis. Use the following formula to calculate it:

$$\text{Depreciation percentage} = \frac{\text{Number of estimated years of life as of beginning of the year}}{\text{Sum of the years' digits}}$$

The following table contains examples of the sum of the years' digits noted in the denominator of the preceding formula:

Total Depreciation Period	Initial Sum of the Years' Digits	Calculation
2 years	3	1 + 2
3 years	6	1 + 2 + 3
4 years	10	1 + 2 + 3 + 4
5 years	15	1 + 2 + 3 + 4 + 5

The concept is illustrated in the following example.

EXAMPLE

Executive Construction buys a motor grader for $10,000. The machine has no estimated salvage value and a useful life of five years. Executive calculates the annual sum of the years' digits depreciation for this machine as:

Year	Number of estimated years of life as of beginning of the year	SYD Calculation	Depreciation Percentage	Annual Depreciation
1	5	5/15	33.33%	$3,333
2	4	4/15	26.67%	2,667
3	3	3/15	20.00%	2,000
4	2	2/15	13.33%	1,333
5	1	1/15	6.67%	667
Totals	15		100.00%	$10,000

Double-Declining Balance Method

The double declining balance (DDB) method is a form of accelerated depreciation. To calculate the double-declining balance depreciation rate, divide the number of years of useful life of an asset into 100 percent, and multiply the result by two. The formula is:

$$(100\% \div \text{Years of useful life}) \times 2$$

The DDB calculation proceeds until the asset's salvage value is reached, after which depreciation ends.

EXAMPLE

Mancuso Construction purchases a small van for $50,000. It has an estimated salvage value of $5,000 and a useful life of five years. The calculation of the double declining balance depreciation rate is:

$$(100\% \div \text{Years of useful life}) \times 2 = 40\%$$

By applying the 40% rate, Mancuso arrives at the following table of depreciation charges per year:

Year	Book Value at Beginning of Year	Depreciation Percentage	DDB Depreciation	Book Value Net of Depreciation
1	$50,000	40%	$20,000	$30,000
2	30,000	40%	12,000	18,000
3	18,000	40%	7,200	10,800
4	10,800	40%	4,320	6,480
5	6,480	40%	1,480	5,000
Total			$45,000	

Note that the depreciation in the fifth and final year is only for $1,480, rather than the $3,240 that would be indicated by the 40% depreciation rate. The reason for the smaller depreciation charge is that Mancuso stops any further depreciation once the remaining book value declines to the amount of the estimated salvage value.

A variation on the double-declining balance method is the 150% method, which substitutes 1.5 for the 2.0 figure used in the calculation. The 150% method does not result in as rapid a rate of depreciation as the double declining method, though the pace of depreciation is still accelerated.

Straight-Line Method

If a company elects not to use accelerated depreciation, it can instead use the straight-line method, where it depreciates an asset at the same standard rate throughout its useful life. Under the straight-line method of depreciation, recognize depreciation expense evenly over the estimated useful life of an asset. The straight-line calculation steps are:
1. Subtract the estimated salvage value of the asset from the amount at which it is recorded on the books.
2. Determine the estimated useful life of the asset. It is easiest to use a standard useful life for each class of assets.
3. Divide the estimated useful life (in years) into 1 to arrive at the straight-line depreciation rate.
4. Multiply the depreciation rate by the asset cost (less salvage value).

EXAMPLE

Energetic Construction buys an online timekeeping system for $6,000. It has an estimated salvage value of $1,000 and a useful life of five years. Energetic calculates the annual straight-line depreciation for the software as:
1. Purchase cost of $6,000 – Estimated salvage value of $1,000 = Depreciable asset cost of $5,000
2. 1 ÷ 5-Year useful life = 20% Depreciation rate per year
3. 20% Depreciation rate × $5,000 Depreciable asset cost = $1,000 Annual depreciation

---

Units of Activity Method

Under the units of activity method, the amount of depreciation charged to expense varies in direct proportion to the amount of asset usage. Thus, more depreciation is charged in periods when there is more asset usage and less depreciation in periods when there is less asset usage. It is the most accurate method for charging depreciation, since it links closely to the wear and tear on assets. However, it also requires the tracking of asset usage, which means that its use is generally limited to more expensive assets. Also, you need to estimate total usage over the life of the asset.

> **Tip:** Do not use the units of activity method if there is not a significant difference in asset usage from period to period. Otherwise, you will spend a great deal of time tracking asset usage and will be rewarded with a depreciation expense that varies little from the results that would have been experienced with the straight-line method (which is far easier to calculate).

Follow these steps to calculate depreciation under the units of activity method:
1. Estimate the total number of hours of usage of the asset, or the total amount of activity to be produced by it over its useful life.
2. Subtract any estimated salvage value from the capitalized cost of the asset and divide the total estimated usage from this net depreciable cost. This yields the depreciation cost per hour of usage or other unit of activity.
3. Multiply the number of hours of usage or units of actual activity by the depreciation cost per hour or unit of activity, which results in the total depreciation expense for the accounting period.

If the estimated number of hours of usage or units of activity changes over time, incorporate these changes into the calculation of the depreciation cost per hour or unit of activity. This will alter the depreciation expense on a go-forward basis.

EXAMPLE

St. Elmo Construction has just purchased a road grader that it uses on construction projects. The cost of the grader was $90,000. The manager of St. Elmo expects to use the grader for 1,000 miles and then sell it off at a salvage value of $40,000, which leaves $50,000 to be depreciated. Since grader usage depends on the presence of client contracts, the manager elects to use the units of activity method for depreciation. Accordingly, the depreciation rate is set at $50 per mile traveled (calculated as $50,000 to be depreciated ÷ 1,000 miles). During the first month of operation, St. Elmo runs the grader for 10 miles, and so charges $500 to depreciation expense.

MACRS Depreciation

MACRS depreciation is the tax depreciation system used in the United States. MACRS is an acronym for Modified Accelerated Cost Recovery System. Under MACRS, fixed assets are assigned to a specific asset class. The Internal Revenue Service has published a complete set of depreciation tables for each of these classes. The classes are noted in the following table. Those assets specifically pertaining to construction activities have been stated in bold.

MACRS Table

Class	Depreciation Period	Description
3-year property	3 years	Tractor units for over-the-road use, race horses over 2 years old when placed in service, any other horse over 12 years old when placed in service, qualified rent-to-own property
5-year property	5 years	Automobiles, taxis, buses, **trucks**, computers and peripheral equipment, office equipment, any property used in research and experimentation, breeding cattle and dairy cattle, appliances and etc. used in residential rental real estate activity, certain green energy property
7-year property	7 years	Office furniture and fixtures, agricultural machinery and equipment, any property not designated as being in another class, natural gas gathering lines
10-year property	10 years	Vessels, barges, tugs, single-purpose agricultural or horticultural structures, trees/vines bearing fruits or nuts, qualified small electric meter and smart electric grid systems
15-year property	15 years	**Certain land improvements (such as shrubbery, fences, roads, sidewalks and bridges)**, retail motor fuel outlets, municipal wastewater treatment plants, clearing and grading land improvements for gas utility property, electric transmission property, natural gas distribution lines

Fixed Asset Accounting

Class	Depreciation Period	Description
20-year property	20 years	Farm buildings (other than those noted under 10-year property), municipal sewers not categorized as 25-year property, the initial clearing and grading of land for electric utility transmission and distribution plants
25-year property	25 years	Property that is an integral part of the water distribution facilities, municipal sewers
Residential rental property	27.5 years	**Any building or structure where 80% or more of its gross rental income is from dwelling units**
Nonresidential real property	39 years	**An office building, store, or warehouse that is not residential property or has a class life of less than 27.5 years**

The depreciation rates associated with the more common asset classes are noted in the following table:

Recovery Year	3-Year Property	5-Year Property	7-Year Property	10-Year Property	15-Year Property	20-Year Property
1	33.33%	20.00%	14.29%	10.00%	5.00%	3.750%
2	44.45%	32.00%	24.49%	18.00%	9.50%	7.219%
3	14.81%	19.20%	17.49%	14.40%	8.55%	6.677%
4	7.41%	11.52%	12.49%	11.52%	7.70%	6.177%
5		11.52%	8.93%	9.22%	6.93%	5.713%
6		5.76%	8.92%	7.37%	6.23%	5.285%
7			8.93%	6.55%	5.90%	4.888%
8			4.46%	6.55%	5.90%	4.522%
9				6.56%	5.91%	4.462%
10				6.55%	5.90%	4.461%
11				3.28%	5.91%	4.462%
12					5.90%	4.461%
13					5.91%	4.462%
14					5.90%	4.461%
15					5.91%	4.462%
16					2.95%	4.461%
17						4.462%
18						4.461%
19						4.462%
20						4.461%
21						2.231%

Depreciation is calculated for tax reporting purposes by aggregating assets into the various classes noted in the preceding table and using the depreciation rates for each class. MACRS ignores salvage value.

The MACRS depreciation rates are used to determine the depreciation expense for taxable income, while the other methods described earlier are used to arrive at the depreciation expense for net income. Since these depreciation methods have differing results, there will be a temporary difference between the book values of fixed assets under the two methods, which will gradually be resolved over their useful lives. Report the difference between depreciation used for calculating taxable income and for the financial statements as a reconciling item in the company's federal income tax return.

The Depreciation of Land

Nearly all fixed assets have a useful life, after which they no longer contribute to the operations of a company or they stop generating revenue. During this useful life, they are depreciated, which reduces their cost to what they are supposed to be worth at the end of their useful lives. Land, however, has no definitive useful life, so there is no way to depreciate it.

The Depreciation of Land Improvements

Land improvements are enhancements to a plot of land to make it more usable. If these improvements have a useful life, depreciate them. If there is no way to estimate a useful life, do not depreciate the cost of the improvements.

If you are preparing land for its intended purpose, include these costs in the cost of the land asset. They are not depreciated. Examples of such costs are:
- Demolishing an existing building
- Clearing and leveling the land

If functionality is being added to the land and the expenditures have a useful life, record them in a separate Land Improvements account. Examples of land improvements are:
- Drainage and irrigation systems
- Fencing
- Landscaping
- Parking lots and walkways

A special item is the ongoing cost of landscaping. This is a period cost, not a fixed asset, and so should be charged to expense as incurred.

EXAMPLE

Quest Construction buys a parcel of land for $1,000,000. Since it is a purchase of land, Quest cannot depreciate the cost. Quest then razes a building that was located on the property at a cost of $25,000, fills in the old foundation for $5,000 and levels the land for $50,000. All of these costs are to prepare the land for its intended purpose, so they are all added to the cost of the land. Quest cannot depreciate these costs.

Quest intends to use the land as a parking lot for its corporate headquarters, so it spends $350,000 to create a parking lot. It estimates that these improvements have a useful life of 10 years. It should record this cost in the Land Improvements account and depreciate it over 10 years.

Depreciation Accounting Entries

The basic depreciation entry is to debit the depreciation expense account (which appears in the income statement) and credit the accumulated depreciation account (which appears in the balance sheet as a contra account that reduces the amount of fixed assets). Over time, the accumulated depreciation balance will continue to increase as more depreciation is added to it, until such time as it equals the original cost of the asset. At that time, stop recording any depreciation expense, since the cost of the asset has now been reduced to zero.

The journal entry for depreciation can be a simple two-line entry designed to accommodate all types of fixed assets, or it may be subdivided into separate entries for each type of fixed asset.

EXAMPLE

Quest Construction calculates that it should have $25,000 of depreciation expense in the current month. The entry is:

	Debit	Credit
Depreciation expense	25,000	
Accumulated depreciation		25,000

In the following month, Quest's accountant decides to show a higher level of precision at the expense account level, and instead elects to apportion the $25,000 of depreciation among different expense accounts, so that each class of asset has a separate depreciation charge. The entry is:

	Debit	Credit
Depreciation expense – Automobiles	4,000	
Depreciation expense – Construction equipment	8,000	
Depreciation expense – Furniture and fixtures	6,000	
Depreciation expense – Office equipment	5,000	
Depreciation expense – Software	2,000	
Accumulated depreciation		25,000

An alternative method for recording depreciation expense is to initially charge the expense pertaining to construction equipment to the equipment ledger, so that depreciation charges are separately accumulated for these items. The entries in the equipment ledger are periodically posted to the general ledger, so this type of depreciation expense will eventually make its way into the financial statements.

Accumulated Depreciation

When an asset is sold or otherwise disposed of, remove all related accumulated depreciation from the accounting records at the same time. Otherwise, an unusually large amount of accumulated depreciation will build up on the balance sheet.

EXAMPLE

Quest Construction has $1,000,000 of fixed assets, for which it has charged $380,000 of accumulated depreciation. This results in the following presentation on Quest's balance sheet:

Fixed assets	$1,000,000
Less: Accumulated depreciation	(380,000)
Net fixed assets	$620,000

Quest then sells equipment for $80,000 that had an original cost of $140,000, and for which it had already recorded accumulated depreciation of $50,000. It records the sale with this journal entry:

	Debit	Credit
Cash	80,000	
Accumulated depreciation	50,000	
Loss on asset sale	10,000	
Fixed assets		140,000

As a result of this entry, Quest's balance sheet presentation of fixed assets has changed, so that fixed assets before accumulated depreciation have declined to $860,000 and accumulated depreciation has declined to $330,000. The new presentation is:

Fixed assets	$860,000
Less: Accumulated depreciation	(330,000)
Net fixed assets	$530,000

The amount of net fixed assets declined by $90,000 as a result of the asset sale, which is the sum of the $80,000 cash proceeds and the $10,000 loss resulting from the asset sale.

Asset Derecognition

An asset is derecognized upon its disposal, or when no future economic benefits can be expected from its use or disposal. Derecognition can arise from a variety of events, such as an asset's sale, scrapping, or donation. The net effect of asset derecognition is to remove an asset and its associated accumulated depreciation from the balance sheet, as well as to recognize any related gain or loss. The gain or loss on derecognition is calculated as the net disposal proceeds, minus the asset's carrying amount.

The asset disposal form is used to formalize the disposition of assets. Ideally, the purchasing department should be involved in disposals, since it presumably has the most experience in obtaining the best prices for goods. Consequently, a large part of the form is set aside for the use of the purchasing staff, which describes how the asset is disposed of and the amount of funds (if any) received. There is space to state billing information, in case the buyer is to be billed. There is also a separate section containing a checklist of activities that the accountant must complete. A sample of the form is presented next.

Abandoned and Idle Assets

If a company abandons an asset, consider the asset to be disposed of and account for it as such (even if it remains on the premises). However, if the asset is only temporarily idle, do not consider it to be abandoned and continue to depreciate it in a normal manner. If an asset has been abandoned, reduce its carrying amount down to any remaining salvage value on the date when the decision is made to abandon the asset.

Some fixed assets will be idle from time to time. There is no specific consideration of idle assets in the accounting standards, so continue to depreciate these assets in the normal manner. However, if an asset is idle, this may indicate that its useful life is shorter than the amount currently used to calculate its depreciation. This may call for a re-evaluation of its useful life.

Sample Asset Disposal Form

Asset Disposal Form

Asset Tag Number	Asset Serial Number	Current Location

Asset Description

Reason for Disposal

☐ No longer usable ☐ Being traded in

☐ Past recommended life span ☐ Lost or stolen*

☐ Being replaced ☐ Other _____

* Contact building security to file a police report

Department Manager Approval Signature

For Use by Purchasing Department

Type of Disposition

☐ Sold ($_____)

☐ Donated

☐ Scrapped

☐ Other _____

If buyer is to be invoiced, state billing information:

Buyer billing information

Purchasing Manager Approval Signature	Disposal Date

For Use by Accounting Department

Accounting Actions Completed

	Initials	Date
☐ Asset removed from general ledger	Initials	Date
☐ Asset removed from equipment register	Initials	Date
☐ Buyer billed for sale amount	Initials	Date
☐ Cash receipt recorded	Initials	Date

Asset Disposal Accounting

There are two scenarios under which a business may dispose of a fixed asset. The first situation arises when a fixed asset is being eliminated without receiving any payment in return. This is a common situation when a fixed asset is being scrapped because it is obsolete or no longer in use and there is no resale market for it. In this case, reverse any accumulated depreciation and reverse the original asset cost. If the asset is fully depreciated, that is the extent of the entry.

EXAMPLE

Quest Construction buys a used backhoe for $10,000 and recognizes $1,000 of depreciation per year over the following ten years. At that time, the machine is not only fully depreciated, but also ready for the scrap heap. Quest gives away the machine for free and records the following entry.

	Debit	Credit
Accumulated depreciation	10,000	
Equipment asset		10,000

A variation on this situation is to write off a fixed asset that has not yet been completely depreciated. In this case, write off the remaining undepreciated amount of the asset to a loss account.

EXAMPLE

To use the same example, Quest gives away the backhoe after eight years, when it has not yet depreciated $2,000 of the asset's original $10,000 cost. In this case, Quest records the following entry:

	Debit	Credit
Loss on asset disposal	2,000	
Accumulated depreciation	8,000	
Equipment asset		10,000

Another scenario arises when an asset is sold, so that the company receives cash in exchange for the fixed asset being sold. Depending upon the price paid and the remaining amount of depreciation that has not yet been charged to expense, this can result in either a gain or a loss on sale of the asset.

EXAMPLE

Quest Construction still disposes of its $10,000 backhoe, but does so after seven years and sells it for $3,500 in cash. In this case, it has already recorded $7,000 of depreciation expense. The entry is:

	Debit	Credit
Cash	3,500	
Accumulated depreciation	7,000	
Gain on asset disposal		500
Equipment asset		10,000

What if Quest had sold the backhoe for $2,500 instead of $3,500? Then there would be a loss of $500 on the sale. The entry would be:

	Debit	Credit
Cash	2,500	
Accumulated depreciation	7,000	
Loss on asset disposal	500	
Machine asset		10,000

The "loss on asset disposal" or "gain on asset disposal" accounts noted in the preceding sample entries are called *disposal accounts*. They may be combined into a single account or used separately to store gains and losses resulting from the disposal of fixed assets.

Summary

From the perspective of the accountant, the tracking of fixed assets can be quite time-consuming. Consequently, we recommend setting a high capitalization limit in order to charge most purchases to expense at once, rather than recording them as fixed assets.

Depreciation is one of the central concerns of the accountant, since the broad range of available methods can result in significant differences in the amount of depreciation expense recorded in each period. Generally, adopt the straight-line depreciation method to minimize the amount of depreciation calculations, unless the usage rate of the assets involved more closely matches a different depreciation method.

Chapter 7
Payables Accounting

Introduction

Accounts payable refers to the aggregate amount of a construction company's short-term obligations to pay suppliers and subcontractors for products and services that the entity purchased on credit. In this chapter, we cover the essentials of accounts payable under the assumption that an accounting software package is in use. This means that a vendor master file is in use, that the accountant has a standard system for assigning names to suppliers and uses an adequate filing system. All of these topics are covered in the following pages, along with discussions of Form 1099 reporting.

Accounting for Accounts Payable

Accounts payable refers to the collective obligation to pay suppliers and subcontractors for goods and services that were acquired on credit. The day-to-day accounting for accounts payable is relatively simple. Whenever the contractor receives an invoice from a supplier, the accountant enters the vendor number of the supplier into the accounting software, which automatically assigns a default general ledger account number from the vendor master file to the invoice. The vendor master file contains essential information about each supplier, including a default account number to which it is assumed that most invoices from that supplier will be charged.

EXAMPLE

Milagro Construction receives an invoice from Milwaukee Electric, which provides the company with electrical power. In the vendor master file, the accountant has already assigned general ledger account number 740, Utilities, to Milwaukee Electric. Thus, when the accountant enters the invoice into the accounts payable module of the accounting software, the system automatically assigns the invoice to account 740.

If the invoice is for goods or services other than the predetermined general ledger account number, the accountant can manually enter a different account number, which is only good for that specific invoice – it does not become the new default account for the supplier. In short, the pre-assignment of account numbers to suppliers greatly simplifies the accounting for payables.

The accounting software should automatically create a credit to the accounts payable account whenever the accountant records a supplier invoice. Thus, a typical entry might be:

	Debit	Credit
Supplies expense [expense account]	xxx	
Accounts payable [liability account]		xxx

Later, when the business pays suppliers (typically during a weekly check run), the accounting system eliminates the accounts payable balance with the following entry:

	Debit	Credit
Accounts payable [liability account]	xxx	
Cash [asset account]		xxx

It is possible that small debit or credit residual balances may appear in the accounts payable account. These balances may be caused by any number of issues, such as credit memos issued by suppliers which the accountant does not plan to use, or amounts that the contractor has valid cause not to pay. Occasionally run the aged accounts payable report to spot these items. Do not use journal entries to clear them out, since this will not be recognized by the report writing software that generates the aged accounts payable report. Instead, always create debit or credit memo transactions that are recognized by the report writer; this will flush the residual balances from the aged accounts payable report.

There is usually an option in the accounting software that automatically generates the necessary debit memo or credit memo. As an example, a contractor may have been granted a credit memo by a supplier for $100, to be used to reduce the amount of an outstanding account payable. The accountant enters the credit memo screen in the accounting software, enters the name of the supplier and the credit memo amount, and selects the expense account that will be offset. The journal entry that the software automatically generates could be as follows:

	Debit	Credit
Accounts payable [liability account]	100	
Supplies expense [expense account]		100

If a supplier offers a discount in exchange for the early payment of an invoice, the accountant is not paying the full amount of the invoice. Instead, that portion of the invoice related to the discount is charged to a separate account. If an accounting software package is used, the system automatically allocates the appropriate amount to this separate account. For example, an entry to take a 2% early payment discount on a supplier invoice might be:

	Debit	Credit
Accounts payable [liability account]	100	
Cash [asset account]		98
Discounts taken [contra expense account]		2

This entry flushes out the full amount of the original account payable, so that no residual balance remains in the accounting records to be paid.

At month-end, it may be necessary to accrue for expenses when goods or services have been received by the business, but for which no supplier invoice has yet been received. To do so, examine the receiving log just after month-end to see which receipts do not have an associated invoice. Also, consider reviewing the expense accruals for the preceding month; a supplier that issues invoices late will probably do so on a repetitive basis, so the last set of expense accruals typically provides clues to what should be included in the next set of accruals.

When a month-end expense accrual is created, it is done with a reversing journal entry, so that the accounting system automatically reverses the expense at the beginning of the following month. Otherwise, the accountant will be at risk of forgetting that an expense was accrued, and may leave it on the books for a number of months. Also, charge the accrued expense to a liability account separate from the accounts payable account, so that all accruals are separately tracked. A common liability account for this is "accrued expenses." Thus, a typical accrued expense entry might be:

	Debit	Credit
Rent expense (expense)	xxx	
Accrued expenses (liability)		xxx

Early Payment Discounts

A key question for the accountant is whether to take early payment terms offered by suppliers. This is a common offer when a supplier is short on cash.

The early payment terms offered by suppliers need to be sufficiently lucrative for the accountant to want to pay invoices early, especially when suppliers are offering such generous terms that the contractor is effectively earning an inordinately high interest rate in exchange for an early payment.

The term structure used for credit terms is to first state the number of days a supplier is giving its customers from the invoice date in which to take advantage of the early payment credit terms. For example, if a customer is supposed to pay within 10 days without a discount, the terms are "net 10 days," whereas if the customer must pay within 10 days to qualify for a 2% discount, the terms are "2/10." Or, if the customer must pay within 10 days to obtain a 2% discount or can make a normal payment in 30 days, then the terms are stated as "2/10 net 30."

The following table shows some of the more common credit terms, explains what they mean, and also notes the effective interest rate being offered to customers with each one.

Sample Credit Terms

Credit Terms	Explanation	Effective Interest
Net 10	Pay in 10 days	None
Net 30	Pay in 30 days	None
Net EOM 10	Pay within 10 days of month-end	None
1/10 net 30	Take a 1% discount if pay in 10 days, otherwise pay in 30 days	18.2%
2/10 net 30	Take a 2% discount if pay in 10 days, otherwise pay in 30 days	36.7%
1/10 net 60	Take a 1% discount if pay in 10 days, otherwise pay in 60 days	7.3%
2/10 net 60	Take a 2% discount if pay in 10 days, otherwise pay in 60 days	14.7%

In case the accountant is dealing with terms different from those shown in the preceding table, it helps to be aware of the formula for calculating the effective interest rate associated with early payment discount terms. The calculation steps are:

1. Calculate the difference between the payment date for those taking the early payment discount and the date when payment is normally due, and divide it into 360 days. For example, under "2/10 net 30" terms, the accountant would divide 20 days into 360 to arrive at 18. Use this number to annualize the interest rate calculated in the next step.

2. Subtract the discount percentage from 100% and divide the result into the discount percentage. For example, under "2/10 net 30" terms, divide 2% by 98% to arrive at 0.0204. This is the interest rate being offered through the credit terms.

3. Multiply the result of both calculations together to obtain the annualized interest rate. To conclude the example, multiply 18 by 0.0204 to arrive at an effective annualized interest rate of 36.72%.

Thus, the full calculation for the cost of credit is:

(Discount % ÷ (1 – Discount %)) × (360 ÷ (Allowed payment days – Discount days))

In general, most early payment discounts represent a sufficiently high effective interest rate that the accountant would be foolish to forego them. However, taking such a discount requires that there be sufficient cash on hand.

The simplest way to ensure that all early payment discounts are accepted and paid in a timely manner is to examine every invoice at the point of initial receipt and set to one side all invoices containing discount offers. This group of invoices containing discounts can then be shifted to a different process flow that emphasizes faster data entry, approval, and payment processing.

If an early payment discount is not taken, be sure to track back through the reasons why the discount was not taken and adjust the processing system to ensure that this does not happen again.

The Vendor Master File

The vendor master file is the central repository of information about each supplier with which a contractor deals. The file is stored within the accounts payable software, and typically contains the following minimum set of information:

- *Supplier identification number.* This is the unique identification number assigned to each supplier by the accountant, and which is used to identify the supplier's record in the payables system.
- *Taxpayer identification number.* This is the identification number assigned to a business by the United States government. This information is needed by the accountant when completing the year-end Form 1099.
- *Supplier name.* This is the legal name of the supplier, and is commonly used as the pay-to name on check payments to suppliers.
- *Supplier DBA name.* In some cases, a company may have a legal name and a different "doing business as" (or DBA) name by which it is more generally known. This name may instead be used as the pay-to name.
- *Supplier address.* This is the administrative address of the supplier, usually where its billing department is located. This address is used to communicate with the billing department of a supplier.
- *Remit to address.* This is the address to which payments are sent to a supplier.
- *Contact phone number.* This is the phone number of the payables department's contact in the billing department of a supplier, to be used if there are questions about a received billing.
- *Early payment discount code.* If a supplier offers a discount for early payments, enter the terms in this field.
- *1099 flag.* If the contractor is required to issue a year-end Form 1099 to a supplier, click on this flag. Doing so will include a supplier in the year-end print run for the Form 1099.
- *Default account.* This is the default expense account to which payments made to the supplier are charged.
- *ACH information.* Separate fields contain room for the supplier's bank routing number and bank account number, as well as the name on the supplier's bank account.

Vendor Master File Usage

The vendor master file is a central component of many payables activities, which is why a high level of record accuracy is needed. Here are several examples of situations in which the file is used:

- *Invoice receipt.* The accountant receives an invoice from a supplier. To enter the invoice in the accounting system for payment, the accountant first does a lookup of supplier names in the vendor master file to find the correct record. Once this record is selected, the system automatically links the new invoice record with the supplier address and early payment discount information (if any) in the vendor master file. The only information that enters the invoice record from the invoice is the invoice date, invoice number, and total amount payable.
- *Supplier payment.* When it is time to pay suppliers, the accounting system draws the amount payable from the invoice record, and the pay-to name and address from the vendor master file. If an ACH payment is being made, the supplier's bank account information is also drawn from the vendor master file.
- *1099 reporting.* At year-end, the contractor may have to issue a completed Form 1099 for certain suppliers. The program in the accounting system that generates these reports uses the 1099 flag in the vendor master file to decide whether a report should be issued at all, and uses the supplier address information and taxpayer identification number in the file to populate the report.

In short, the vendor master file contains a large amount of information about suppliers that is central to the efficient functioning of the accountant.

A supplier may not necessarily be set up with a record in the vendor master file. This is most likely to be the case when there is an expectation that a supplier will only be used once. In this case, it may be more efficient to enter all necessary payment information in a separate data entry form in the payables software. The result will be a single invoice record that contains all information needed to pay a supplier. If such an entity were to become a more frequent supplier with regular billings, it would then make more sense to create a unique record for it in the vendor master file.

Supplier Naming Conventions

It is important to avoid creating a new record in the vendor master file for suppliers that already have an existing record. Otherwise, the accountant will assign some supplier invoices to one version of a master file record and some invoices to a different version. This can lead to the following situations:

- *Duplicate payment.* An invoice is initially submitted and recorded under one version of the supplier record; the invoice payment is late in arriving, so the supplier sends a duplicate invoice, which is recorded under a different version of the supplier record. The result is that the second invoice is not flagged by the software as being a duplicate invoice, so the contractor pays the supplier twice.

- *Incomplete records.* The accounting system reveals an incomplete list of billings from a supplier, since some billings are linked to a different supplier record.
- *Incorrect 1099.* A year-end Form 1099 is completed that does not contain the total amount paid to a supplier, since the payments are split among different records.
- *Missing address update.* A supplier submits an address change, but the change is only updated on one of its record versions, resulting in some old invoices being paid to an old pay-to address.

To avoid these problems, it is necessary to create and follow a rigidly-defined naming convention. A naming convention sets forth rules for how to create a supplier identification number. For example, the name of a new supplier for a contractor is The Flooring Specialist. When developing an identification number, the following problems arise:

- Should the identification number start with "The" or with "Flooring"?
- How much of this long supplier name should be included in the identification number?

The usual naming convention would drop "The" from the identification number and probably truncate the name after five or six characters. By employing these rules, the supplier identification number would become either FLOOR (five characters) or FLOORI (six characters).

How should a naming convention deal with several suppliers whose names begin with the same characters? The convention usually allows for the sequential numbering of these additional suppliers. For example, the first supplier that a contractor has is The Flooring Company, so the preceding naming convention indicates that the supplier identification number should be FLOOR001. A year later, the contractor takes on a supplier with the somewhat similar name of Flooring Specialists. Under the terms of the naming convention, the identification number assigned to this supplier will be FLOOR002.

There may be a need for a number of additional naming conventions to deal with unusual supplier names, such as:

- Eliminate all spaces from supplier names. For example, Jones and Smith could be interpreted as JONESAN001.
- Drop all periods from a name. For example, I.D.C. Corporation could be interpreted as IDCCO001.
- Use an ampersand (&) instead of "and" in a name. To return to the preceding Jones and Smith supplier name, it could be interpreted as JONES&S. Doing so leaves more room to introduce additional characters that could uniquely identify a supplier.

- Use the last name of an individual. For example, the contractor pays a private contractor named John Arbuckle. There are many contractors named John, so the identification number instead uses the last name to derive AR-BUC001.

The Payables Filing System

The payables function is one of the largest generators of paperwork in a business. It should be organized to meet the following two goals:
- To make documents easily accessible for payment purposes
- To make documents easily accessible for auditors

The second requirement, to have paperwork available for auditors, does not just refer to the auditors who examine the contractor's financial statements at year-end. In addition, the local government may send use tax auditors who will also review the records. Consider maintaining the following systems of records to meet the preceding needs:
- *Supplier files*. There should be one file for each supplier that has been paid within the past year. Within each file, staple all paid invoices and related documents to the remittance advice for each paid check. These checks should be filed by date, with the most recent payment in front.
- *Unpaid invoices file*. There should be a separate file of unpaid invoices, which is usually sorted alphabetically by the name of the supplier. If there is more than one unpaid invoice for a supplier, sort them by date for each supplier.
- *Unmatched documents file*. If the firm is using three-way matching, have separate files for unmatched invoices, purchase orders, and receiving documentation. Three-way matching refers to comparing a supplier invoice to an authorizing purchase order and receiving documentation before paying the supplier.

> **Tip:** It is not necessary to maintain a separate supplier folder for every supplier. If a supplier only issues invoices a few times a year, include them in an "Other" folder that applies to a letter range of suppliers. For example, there may be an "Other A-C" folder, followed by an "Other D-F" folder, and so forth. Review these "Other" folders periodically, extract the invoices of any suppliers that are generating an increasing volume of invoices, and prepare separate folders for these suppliers.

Government Reporting

The key government reporting requirement for payables is the provision of the Form 1099 to the government following the end of each calendar year. In this section, we describe the contents of this form, the use of the Form W-9 to obtain the identification information used on the Form 1099 and several related topics.

The Form 1099-MISC

The Form 1099-MISC contains the aggregate amount of cash payments made to a supplier in the preceding calendar year. The IRS uses this document to confirm the amount of income that each supplier reports on its annual tax return. Depending on the type of payment made, it is usually not necessary to issue the form if the cumulative cash payments to a supplier for the full calendar year are less than $600.

The form is sent to the Internal Revenue Service (IRS) and the supplier by early February of the following year, or with the IRS by the end of March if the form is filed electronically. The form copies are distributed as follows:

- Copy A to the IRS
- Copy B to the recipient (supplier)
- Copy C to be retained by the business
- Copy 1 to the state tax department
- Copy 2 to the recipient (supplier) to file with its state income tax return

The filing period can be extended 30 days by requesting an extension on IRS Form 8809 (which is available as an on-line form).

The 1099 vendor designation should be applied to any supplier that has the following characteristics (this is a partial list):

- Commissions paid to non-employees
- Director's fees
- Fees paid to independent contractors
- Fish purchased for cash
- Golden parachute payments
- Professional services fees
- Taxable fringe benefits for non-employees

Generally, this designation is for a supplier entity that is not a corporation. A sample Form 1099-MISC follows.

Sample Form 1099-MISC

Explanations of the key boxes on the form are noted in the following table; we have not described boxes that are entirely unrelated to the construction industry.

Contents of Key 1099-MISC Fields

Box Number	Box Description
Box 1	Rent – Includes real estate rentals paid for office space, unless they were paid to a real estate agent. Also includes machine rentals. The minimum reporting threshold is $600.
Box 2	Royalties – Includes gross royalty payments, such as from patents, copyrights, trade names, and trademarks. The minimum reporting threshold is $10.
Box 3	Other income – Includes other income of at least $600 that is not reportable under any of the other boxes on the form.
Box 4	Federal income tax withheld – Includes any backup withholdings made on payments to suppliers.
Box 6	Medical and health care payments – Includes payments to each physician or other provider of medical or health care services. The minimum reporting threshold is $600.

Box Number	Box Description
Box 7	Nonemployee compensation – Includes fees, commissions, prizes and awards paid to non-employees, and other forms of compensation for services performed. The minimum reporting threshold is $600.
Box 8	Substitute payments in lieu of dividends or interest – These are payments made in place of dividends or interest to the extent that interest accrued while securities were on loan. The minimum reporting threshold is $10.
Box 14	Gross proceeds paid to an attorney – Includes amounts paid to an attorney for legal services. The minimum reporting threshold is $600.

On the form, Box 7 is most commonly used to report payments made to suppliers and subcontractors.

When submitting 1099s to the federal government, also include a Form 1096 transmittal return, which is essentially a cover letter that identifies the entity providing the forms. A sample Form 1096 follows.

Sample Form 1096

Treatment of Incorrect Filings

It is unfortunately common for a Form 1099 to contain incorrect information. In this section, we describe how to provide corrected information to the IRS, as well as how to deal with recalcitrant suppliers who do not provide correct identification information to the company.

If the amount paid or payee name information on a Form 1099 is found to be incorrect, create a replacement form, check the "Corrected" box at the top of the form, and enter the correct information.

If the TIN number on a Form 1099 is found to be incorrect, create a replacement form, check the "Corrected" box at the top of the form, and enter the payer, recipient, and account number information as it appeared on the original incorrect return, with the amount paid set at zero; this deletes the original filing. Then prepare and submit a new Form 1099 with the correct TIN included, which will replace the original filing.

If 1099s are sent to the IRS and the IRS finds that one or more of the TINs on these forms are incorrect, it will send a notification to the organization, detailing which TINs are incorrect. Upon receipt of this document, the accountant must send a "B" notice and a Form W-9 (see the next sub-section) to each indicated supplier within the later of the next 15 business days or the date of the IRS notice. A "B" notice is a backup withholding notice. The first of these notices contains the following statements:

- The supplier's TIN does not match the IRS' records
- If a correct TIN is not provided, the business will be required to withhold from future payments to the supplier and remit these funds to the IRS
- There may also be a penalty
- What the supplier has to do to correct the situation
- The supplier is required to send the firm a signed Form W-9 before the due date stated on the notice

If the company receives a second notification from the IRS, it must send a second "B" notice to the indicated suppliers. This second notice again warns the supplier of the firm's obligation to begin backup withholdings and tells the supplier to contact the IRS to obtain a correct TIN. This notice does not need to include another Form W-9.

The Form W-9

A contractor needs accurate identification information about each of its suppliers before it can submit the Form 1099 to the government. To collect this information, have all suppliers submit a Form W-9, Request for Taxpayer Identification Number and Certification. A sample Form W-9 follows.

Sample Form W-9

Form **W-9** (Rev. August 2013) Department of the Treasury Internal Revenue Service	**Request for Taxpayer Identification Number and Certification**	**Give Form to the requester. Do not send to the IRS.**

Name (as shown on your income tax return)
Wilson Brothers Office Supplies

Business name/disregarded entity name, if different from above

Check appropriate box for federal tax classification:
☐ Individual/sole proprietor   ☑ C Corporation   ☐ S Corporation   ☐ Partnership   ☐ Trust/estate
☐ Limited liability company. Enter the tax classification (C=C corporation, S=S corporation, P=partnership) ▶ _____
☐ Other (see instructions) ▶

Exemptions (see instructions):
Exempt payee code (if any) _____
Exemption from FATCA reporting code (if any) _____

Address (number, street, and apt. or suite no.)
567 Wilfred Avenue
City, state, and ZIP code
Denver, CO 80202

Requester's name and address (optional)

List account number(s) here (optional)

Part I   Taxpayer Identification Number (TIN)

Enter your TIN in the appropriate box. The TIN provided must match the name given on the "Name" line to avoid backup withholding. For individuals, this is your social security number (SSN). However, for a resident alien, sole proprietor, or disregarded entity, see the Part I instructions on page 3. For other entities, it is your employer identification number (EIN). If you do not have a number, see *How to get a TIN* on page 3.

Note. If the account is in more than one name, see the chart on page 4 for guidelines on whose number to enter.

Social security number

Employer identification number
8 4 – 9 8 7 6 5 4 3

Part II   Certification

Under penalties of perjury, I certify that:

1. The number shown on this form is my correct taxpayer identification number (or I am waiting for a number to be issued to me), and

2. I am not subject to backup withholding because: (a) I am exempt from backup withholding, or (b) I have not been notified by the Internal Revenue Service (IRS) that I am subject to backup withholding as a result of a failure to report all interest or dividends, or (c) the IRS has notified me that I am no longer subject to backup withholding, and

3. I am a U.S. citizen or other U.S. person (defined below), and

4. The FATCA code(s) entered on this form (if any) indicating that I am exempt from FATCA reporting is correct.

Certification instructions. You must cross out item 2 above if you have been notified by the IRS that you are currently subject to backup withholding because you have failed to report all interest and dividends on your tax return. For real estate transactions, item 2 does not apply. For mortgage interest paid, acquisition or abandonment of secured property, cancellation of debt, contributions to an individual retirement arrangement (IRA), and generally, payments other than interest and dividends, you are not required to sign the certification, but you must provide your correct TIN. See the instructions on page 3.

Sign Here | Signature of U.S. person ▶ | Date ▶

It is a good practice to have the Form W-9 updated on an annual basis, in order to have the most recent mailing address on file for each supplier. Doing so also warns of any organizational changes in a supplier. However, this can be difficult if there are many suppliers. Usually, a simple e-mail notice to each supplier to ask for a revised Form W-9 if there have been any informational changes is considered sufficient.

Summary

The accountant must deal with accounts payable in a highly organized manner. Otherwise, there is a good chance that suppliers will be paid too late, not at all, or more than once – none of which are good for the reputation of the business. When these situations occur on a regular basis, suppliers are more likely to withdraw credit, leaving a company to pay up-front with cash. Consequently, payables is the first place in which to create rigid procedures, filing standards, and calendars of activities.

Chapter 8
Debt Accounting

Introduction

A contractor may not have a sufficient amount of funds on hand to pay for a construction project, and so must borrow funds from a lender to bridge the funding gap. This may result in a contractor having a number of loans available, each one associated with a different project.

The accounting for debt is not especially difficult, since the accounting entries needed are fairly simple. However, it is necessary to determine the interest component of each debt payment, so that the contractor properly presents in its balance sheet the correct amount of remaining debt outstanding.

In this chapter, we address the classification of and accounting for debt, as well as the concept of the amortization schedule and the need to periodically reconcile the debt account. In addition, we describe the concept of a participating mortgage loan, where the lender can participate in the results of a project.

Basic Debt Accounting

Debt is defined as an amount owed for funds borrowed. This may take a variety of forms, such as:

- Credit card debt, which can either be paid off each month or carried forward in exchange for a high interest rate.
- A line of credit, which is used to meet short-term needs, and which is usually limited to the amount of collateral that the contractor has available to guarantee repayment.
- A promissory note, which is a fixed sum that a contractor borrows and then commits to pay back over time, in accordance with a fixed repayment schedule.

There are several issues that the borrower must be aware of when accounting for debt. The initial issue is how to classify the debt in the accounting records. Here are the main areas to be concerned with:

- If the debt is payable within one year, record the debt in a short-term debt account; this is a liability account. The typical line of credit is payable within one year, and so is classified as short-term debt.
- If the debt is payable in more than one year, record the debt in a long-term debt account; this is a liability account.
- If a loan agreement contains a clause stating that the lender can demand payment at any time, classify the debt as a current liability. This is the case

even if there is no expectation that the lender will demand payment within the current year.

- If the debt is in the form of a credit card statement, this is typically handled as an account payable, and so is simply recorded through the accounts payable module in the accounting software.

The next debt accounting issue is how to determine the amount of interest expense associated with debt. This is usually quite easy, since the lender includes the amount of the interest expense on its periodic billing statements to the contractor. In the case of a line of credit, the borrower is probably required to maintain its primary checking account with the lending bank, so the bank simply deducts the interest from the checking account once a month. This amount is usually identified as an interest charge on the monthly bank statement, so the accountant can easily identify it and record it as part of the monthly bank reconciliation adjustments. Alternatively, the lender may provide an amortization schedule to the borrower, which states the proportions of interest expense and loan repayment that will comprise each subsequent payment made to the lender. See the next section for a description of an amortization schedule.

The next issue is how to account for the various debt-related transactions. They are as follows:

- *Initial loan.* When a loan is first taken out, debit the cash account and credit either the short-term debt account or long-term debt account, depending on the nature of the loan. For example, a contractor borrows $1,000,000. The entry is:

	Debit	Credit
Cash [asset account]	1,000,000	
Long-term debt [liability account]		1,000,000

- *Interest payment.* If there is no immediate loan repayment, with only interest being paid, then the entry is a debit to the interest expense account and a credit to the cash account. For example, the interest rate on the $1,000,000 just described is 7%, with payments due at the end of each year. After one year, the entry is:

	Debit	Credit
Interest expense [expense account]	70,000	
Cash [asset account]		70,000

- *Mixed payment.* If a payment is being made that includes both interest expense and a loan repayment, debit the interest expense account, debit the applicable loan liability account, and credit the cash account. For example, a

$5,000 loan payment is comprised of $4,300 of interest expense and $700 of loan repayment. The entry is:

	Debit	Credit
Interest expense [expense account]	4,300	
Short-term debt [liability account]	700	
Cash [asset account]		5,000

- *Final payment.* If there is a final balloon payment where most or all of the debt is repaid, debit the applicable loan liability account and credit the cash account. For example, a contractor has been paying nothing but interest on a $500,000 loan for the past four years, and now repays the entire loan balance. The entry is:

	Debit	Credit
Short-term debt [liability account]	500,000	
Cash [asset account]		500,000

The Amortization Schedule

An amortization schedule is a table that states the periodic payments to be made as part of a loan agreement, and which notes the following information on each line of the table:

- Payment number
- Payment due date
- Payment total
- Interest component of payment
- Principal component of payment
- Ending principal balance remaining

Thus, the calculation on each line of the amortization schedule is designed to arrive at the ending principal balance for each period, for which the calculation is:

Beginning principal balance - (Payment total - Interest expense) = Ending principal balance

The amortization schedule is extremely useful for accounting for each payment in a promissory note, since it separates the interest and principal components of each payment. The schedule is also useful for modeling how the remaining loan liability will vary if you accelerate or delay payments or alter their size. An amortization schedule can also encompass balloon payments and even negative amortization situations where the principal balance increases over time.

A sample amortization schedule follows, where a borrower has taken on a $50,000 loan that is to be repaid with five annual payments, using an interest rate of

8%. Note how the proportion of interest expense to the total payment made rapidly declines, until there is almost no interest expense remaining in the final payment. The schedule also notes the total interest expense associated with the loan.

Sample Amortization Schedule

Year	Beginning Loan Balance	Loan Payment	8% Interest	Loan Repayment	Ending Loan Balance
1	$50,000	$12,523	$4,000	$8,523	$41,477
2	41,477	12,523	3,318	9,205	32,272
3	32,272	12,523	2,582	9,941	22,331
4	22,331	12,523	1,786	10,737	11,594
5	11,594	12,522	928	11,594	0
		$62,614	$12,614	$50,000	

* Note: The Year 5 payment was reduced by $1 to offset the effects of rounding.

Reconciling the Debt Account

It is essential for the accountant to periodically compare the remaining loan balance reported by the lender to the balance reported on the books of the company. It is entirely possible that there will be a difference, for which there are usually two reasons. They are:

- The loan payments made by the borrower to the lender arrived either earlier or later than the payment due date. This alters the amount of interest expense charged to the borrower.
- The most recent loan payment made by the borrower to the lender is still in transit to the lender, or has not yet been recorded by the lender in its accounting system.

If there is a difference, contact the lender and determine the nature of the difference. If the interest charge recognized by the lender varies from the amount recognized by the borrower, alter the borrower's interest expense to match the amount recognized by the lender. If the difference is due to a payment in transit, no adjustment to the accounting records needs to be made.

The reason why this reconciliation is so necessary is that the contractor's auditors will contact the lender at the end of the year to confirm with them the amount owed by the contractor. If the auditors discover a difference, they will require the contractor to adjust its loan records.

Participating Mortgage Loans

A participating mortgage loan is one in which the lender can participate in the results of operations of the real estate operation being mortgaged, or in any appreciation in the market value of the real estate.

Debt Accounting

The borrower should account for a participating mortgage loan by recognizing a participation liability that is based on the fair value of the participation feature at the start of the loan. The offset to this liability is the debt discount account. Subsequently, the accountant should account for the following issues related to the participating mortgage loan:

- *Interest.* Charge to expense any periodic interest expense amounts so designated in the mortgage agreement.
- *Amortization.* Amortize the amount of the debt discount related to the lender's participation in the profits of the real estate venture.
- *Participation payments.* Pay the lender for its share of profits of the real estate venture, and charge this amount to interest expense. The offset is to the participation liability account.
- *Participation adjustment.* At the end of each reporting period, adjust the participation liability to match the latest fair value of the participation feature.

If the mortgage loan is extinguished prior to its due date, recognize a debt extinguishment gain or loss on the difference between the recorded amount of the debt and the amount paid or exchanged to settle the debt liability.

EXAMPLE

Domicilio Corporation develops residential real estate in the Miami area. On April 1, 20X1, Domicilio buys a property for $20,000,000. Domicilio obtains the funding for this purchase primarily with a $15 million participating mortgage loan from Primero Bank. The loan agreement is for four years, and requires interest-only payments at a 6% interest rate, until a balloon payment is required at the end of the loan term. In addition, Primero will receive a 10% participation in the profits from the sale of each residential unit, payable at the maturity of the loan.

The initial estimate of the fair value of the participation feature is $60,000, so Domicilio records the following initial entry for the loan:

	Debit	Credit
Cash	15,000,000	
Loan discount	60,000	
Mortgage loan payable		15,000,000
Participation liability		60,000

At the end of one year, Domicilio records the following entry related to the interest expense paid on the mortgage and the straight-line amortization of the discount on the mortgage:

	Debit	Credit
Interest expense	915,000	
Cash		900,000
Loan discount		15,000

Midway through the next year, Domicilio adjusts its estimate of the fair value of the participation feature upward by $22,000. This results in the following entry:

	Debit	Credit
Loan discount	22,000	
Participation liability		22,000

Thus, 18 months into the participating mortgage loan, the participation liability recorded by Domicilio has increased to $82,000, while the balance in the loan discount account has increased to $67,000.

Summary

Though debt accounting should not be especially difficult, we must emphasize the need to reconcile the debt account at regular intervals. This is an area in which the amounts of interest recognized by the lender and borrower can easily diverge, resulting in notable differences. It is better to locate and eliminate these differences prior to year-end, rather than having the auditors discover them.

Chapter 9
Contingencies

Introduction

A contractor may sometimes find it necessary to record a loss in anticipation of a future event that has not yet been settled, usually in regard to a dispute with a client over a change order or claim. Or, it may want to record a gain in relation to a future event. While the first event is all too common, the latter event is essentially prohibited. In this chapter, we discuss when and how to account for and disclose contingencies.

Loss Contingencies

A loss contingency arises when there is a situation for which the outcome is uncertain, and which should be resolved in the future, possibly creating a loss. Examples of contingent loss situations are:

- A contractor builds an especially robust parking garage that exceeds the requirements of the client and has filed a claim to recover the excess cost of this change; the claim is likely to fail, so the contractor will incur a loss.
- A client threatens a lawsuit over a failed construction project.

When deciding whether to account for a loss contingency, the basic concept is to only record a loss that is probable and for which the amount of the loss can be reasonably estimated. If the best estimate of the amount of the loss is within a range, accrue whichever amount appears to be a better estimate than the other estimates in the range. If there is no "better estimate" in the range, accrue a loss for the minimum amount in the range.

If it is not possible to arrive at a reasonable estimate of the loss associated with an event, only disclose the existence of the contingency in the notes accompanying the financial statements. Or, if it is not probable that a loss will be incurred, even if it is possible to estimate the amount of a loss, only disclose the circumstances of the contingency, without accruing a loss.

EXAMPLE

Armadillo Construction has been notified by the local zoning commission that it must remediate abandoned property on which chemicals had been stored in the past. Armadillo has hired a consulting firm to estimate the cost of remediation, which has been documented at $10 million. Since the amount of the loss has been reasonably estimated and it is probable that the loss will occur, the company can record the $10 million as a contingent loss. If the zoning commission had not indicated the company's liability, it may have been more appropriate to only mention the loss in the disclosures accompanying the financial statements.

EXAMPLE

Armadillo Construction has been notified that a third party may begin legal proceedings against it, based on a situation involving environmental damage to a site on which work was once performed by Armadillo. Based on the experience of other companies who have been subjected to this type of litigation, it is probable that Armadillo will have to pay $8 million to settle the litigation. A separate aspect of the litigation is still open to interpretation, but could potentially require an additional $12 million to settle. Given the current situation, Armadillo should accrue a loss in the amount of $8 million for that portion of the situation for which the outcome is probable, and for which the amount of the loss can be reasonably estimated.

If the conditions for recording a loss contingency are initially not met, but then are met during a later accounting period, the loss should be accrued in the later period. Do not make a retroactive adjustment to an earlier period to record a loss contingency.

Gain Contingencies

The accounting standards do not allow the recognition of a gain contingency, since doing so might result in the recognition of revenue before the contingent event has been settled.

Contingency Disclosures

When a loss accrual is made that relates to a loss contingency, it may be necessary to disclose the nature of the accrual and the amount accrued, in order to keep the financial statements from being misleading. The accounting standards do not allow an organization to use the word "reserve" when describing a loss contingency, since it implies that a business has set aside funds to deal with a contingency – which may not be the case.

If it is not possible to estimate the amount of a loss contingency, but there is a reasonable possibility that a loss has been incurred, the contractor should disclose:
- The nature of the contingency
- A statement that a loss estimate cannot be made, or the range of the possible loss

If a claim or assessment has not yet been asserted against a business, there is no need to disclose a loss contingency. However, disclosure must be made if it is probable that a claim will be asserted, and that there is a reasonable possibility of an unfavorable outcome.

In those rare cases where a reasonably-estimated loss contingency arises after the date of the financial statements, it may make sense to add pro forma financial information to the financial statements, showing the effect on the business if the loss had arisen during the reporting period.

EXAMPLE

Armadillo Construction is engaged in settlement discussions with a plaintiff regarding an environmental damages lawsuit. Armadillo makes the following disclosure:

> Armadillo is currently engaged in settlement discussions with a plaintiff in a lawsuit involving the amount of environmental mitigation activities needed for a property that Armadillo recently sold to the plaintiff. The company's current settlement offer is $10 million, while the plaintiff's offer is $30 million. Armadillo's estimate of this liability is a range between the two offers, with no amount in the range considered a better estimate than any other amount. Accordingly, the company has accrued a $10 million loss.

If a contingency may result in a gain, it is allowable to disclose the nature of the contingency. However, the disclosure should not make any potentially misleading statements about the likelihood of realization of the contingent gain.

Summary

The accounting for contingencies is rarely completely clear. Instead, the probability associated with a future event is gradually clarified over time, as is the amount of the associated loss. Accordingly, the accountant will likely have to monitor the circumstances of each contingent event over time and make decisions regarding when to begin disclosing a contingency, and then later the amount to accrue if the event becomes more probable. The result may well be continuing revisions to the amount of a loss contingency, until such time as the exact amount is settled and paid out.

Chapter 10
Lease Accounting

Introduction

A construction company may elect to lease equipment rather than purchasing it. This is a reasonable choice when the firm does not have enough cash to make an outright purchase. The accounting for leases has become much more complex in recent years, to the point where the average accountant could have quite a difficult time presenting the correct lease-related information in the financial statements. In this chapter, we cover the basics of lease accounting – but keep in mind that an entire book or course may be needed to gain a complete understanding of this topic.

The Nature of a Lease

A lease is an arrangement under which a lessor agrees to allow a lessee to control the use of identified property, plant, and equipment for a stated period of time in exchange for one or more payments. A lease arrangement is quite a useful opportunity, for the following reasons:

- The lessee reduces its exposure to asset ownership
- The lessee obtains financing from the lessor in order to pay for the asset
- The lessee now has access to the leased asset

An arrangement is considered to give control over the use of an asset when both of these conditions are present:

- The lessee obtains the right to substantially all of the economic benefits from using an asset; and
- The lessee obtains the right to direct the uses to which an asset is put.

Lease Types

It is critical to determine the type of a lease, since the accounting varies by lease type. The choices are that a lease can be designated as either a finance lease or an operating lease. In essence, a *finance lease* designation implies that the lessee has purchased the underlying asset (even though this may not actually be the case) while an *operating lease* designation implies that the lessee has obtained the use of the underlying asset for only a period of time. A lessee should classify a lease as a finance lease when any of the following criteria are met:

- *Ownership transfer*. Ownership of the underlying asset is shifted to the lessee by the end of the lease term.
- *Ownership option*. The lessee has a purchase option to buy the leased asset and is reasonably certain to use it.

- *Lease term.* The lease term covers the major part of the underlying asset's remaining economic life. This is considered to be 75% or more of the remaining economic life of the underlying asset. This criterion is not valid if the lease commencement date is near the end of the asset's economic life, which is considered to be a date that falls within the last 25% of the underlying asset's total economic life.
- *Present value.* The present value of the sum of all lease payments and any lessee-guaranteed residual value matches or exceeds the fair value of the underlying asset. The present value is based on the interest rate implicit in the lease.
- *Specialization.* The asset is so specialized that it has no alternative use for the lessor following the lease term. In this situation, there are essentially no remaining benefits that revert to the lessor.

When none of the preceding criteria are met, the lessee must classify a lease as an operating lease.

A central concept of the accounting for leases is that the lessee should recognize the assets and liabilities that underlie each leasing arrangement. This concept results in the following recognition in the balance sheet of the lessee as of the lease commencement date:
- Recognize a liability to make lease payments to the lessor
- Recognize a right-of-use asset that represents the right of the lessee to use the leased asset during the lease term

There are a number of sub-topics related to asset and liability recognition for a lease, which are stated in the following sections.

Initial Lease Measurement

As of the commencement date of a lease, the lessee measures the liability and the right-of-use asset associated with the lease. These measurements are derived as follows:
- *Lease liability.* The present value of the lease payments, discounted at the discount rate for the lease. This rate is the rate implicit in the lease when that rate is readily determinable. If not, the lessee instead uses its incremental borrowing rate.
- *Right-of-use asset.* The initial amount of the lease liability, plus any lease payments made to the lessor before the lease commencement date, plus any initial direct costs incurred, minus any lease incentives received.

EXAMPLE

Inscrutable Construction enters into a five-year lease, where the lease payments are $35,000 per year, payable at the end of each year. Inscrutable incurs initial direct costs of $8,000. The rate implicit in the lease is 8%.

At the commencement of the lease, the lease liability is $139,745, which is calculated as $35,000 multiplied by the 3.9927 rate for the five-period present value of an ordinary annuity. The right-of-use asset is calculated as the lease liability plus the amount of the initial direct costs, for a total of $147,745.

Short-Term Leases

When a lease has a term of 12 months or less, the lessee can elect not to recognize lease-related assets and liabilities in the balance sheet. This election is made by class of asset. When a lessee makes this election, it should usually recognize the expense related to a lease on a straight-line basis over the term of the lease.

If the lease term changes so that the remaining term now extends more than 12 months beyond the end of the previously determined lease term or the lessee will likely purchase the underlying asset, the arrangement is no longer considered a short-term lease. In this situation, account for the lease as a longer-term lease as of the date when there was a change in circumstances.

Finance Leases

When a lessee has designated a lease as a finance lease, it should recognize the following over the term of the lease:
- The ongoing amortization of the right-of-use asset
- The ongoing amortization of the interest on the lease liability
- Any variable lease payments that are not included in the lease liability
- Any impairment of the right-of-use asset

The amortization period for the right-of-use asset is from the lease commencement date to the earlier of the end of the lease term or the end of the useful life of the asset. An exception is when it is reasonably certain that the lessee will exercise an option to purchase the asset, in which case the amortization period is through the end of the asset's useful life.

After the commencement date, the lessee increases the carrying amount of the lease liability to include the interest expense on the lease liability, while reducing the carrying amount by the amount of all lease payments made during the period. The interest on the lease liability is the amount that generates a constant periodic discount rate on the remaining liability balance.

After the commencement date, the lessee reduces the right-of-use asset by the amount of accumulated amortization and accumulated impairment (if any).

EXAMPLE

Giro Construction agrees to a five-year lease of equipment that requires an annual $20,000 payment, due at the end of each year. At the end of the lease period, Giro has the option to buy the equipment for $1,000. Since the expected residual value of the equipment at that time is expected to be $25,000, the large discount makes it reasonably certain that the purchase option will be exercised. At the commencement date of the lease, the fair value of the equipment is $120,000, with an economic life of eight years. The discount rate for the lease is 6%.

Giro classifies the lease as a finance lease, since it is reasonably certain to exercise the purchase option.

The lease liability at the commencement date is $84,995, which is calculated as the present value of five payments of $20,000, plus the present value of the $1,000 purchase option payment, discounted at 6%. Giro recognizes the right-of-use asset as the same amount, since there are no initial direct costs, lease incentives, or other types of payments made by Giro, either at or before the commencement date.

Giro amortizes the right-of-use asset over the eight-year expected useful life of the equipment, under the assumption that it will exercise the purchase option and therefore keep the equipment for the eight-year period.

As an example of the subsequent accounting for the lease, Giro recognizes a first-year interest expense of $5,100 (calculated as 6% × $84,995 lease liability), and recognizes the amortization of the right-of-use asset in the amount of $10,624 (calculated as $84,995 ÷ 8 years). This results in a lease liability at the end of Year 1 that has been reduced to $70,095 (calculated as $84,995 + $5,100 interest - $20,000 lease payment) and a right-of-use asset that has been reduced to $74,371 (calculated as $84,995 - $10,624 amortization).

By the end of Year 5, which is when the lease terminates, the lease liability has been reduced to $1,000, which is the amount of the purchase option. Giro exercises the option, which settles the remaining liability. At that time, the carrying amount of the right-of-use asset has declined to $31,875 (reflecting five years of amortization at $10,624 per year). Giro shifts this amount into a fixed asset account and depreciates it over the remaining three years of its useful life.

Operating Leases

When a lessee has designated a lease as an operating lease, the lessee should recognize the following over the term of the lease:
- A lease cost in each period, where the total cost of the lease is allocated over the lease term on a straight-line basis. This can be altered if there is another systematic and rational basis of allocation that more closely follows the benefit usage pattern to be derived from the underlying asset.
- Any variable lease payments that are not included in the lease liability
- Any impairment of the right-of-use asset

A leasehold improvement asset should be amortized over the *shorter* of the remaining lease term and its useful life.

EXAMPLE

Nuance Construction enters into an operating lease in which the lease payment is $25,000 per year for the first five years and $30,000 per year for the next five years. These payments sum to $275,000 over ten years. Nuance will therefore recognize a lease expense of $27,500 per year for all of the years in the lease term.

At any point in the life of an operating lease, the remaining cost of the lease is considered to be the total lease payments, plus all initial direct costs associated with the lease, minus the lease cost already recognized in previous periods.

After the commencement date, the lessee measures the lease liability at the present value of the lease payments that have not yet been made, using the same discount rate that was established at the commencement date.

After the commencement date, the lessee measures the right-of-use asset at the amount of the lease liability, adjusted for the following items:
- Any impairment of the asset
- Prepaid or accrued lease payments
- Any remaining balance of lease incentives received
- Any unamortized initial direct costs

EXAMPLE

Hubble Construction enters into a 10-year operating lease for its corporate offices. The annual lease payment is $40,000 to be paid at the end of each year. The company incurs initial direct costs of $8,000, and receives $15,000 from the lessor as a lease incentive. Hubble's incremental borrowing rate is 6%. The initial direct costs and lease incentive will be amortized over the 10 years of the lease term.

Hubble measures the lease liability as the present value of the 10 lease payments at a 6% discount rate, which is $294,404. The right-of-use asset is measured at $287,404, which is the initial $294,404 measurement, plus the initial direct costs of $8,000, minus the lease incentive of $15,000.

After one year, the carrying amount of the lease liability is $272,068, which is the present value of the remaining nine lease payments at a 6% discount rate. The carrying amount of the right-of-use asset is $265,768, which is the amount of the liability, plus the unamortized initial direct costs of $7,200, minus the remaining balance of the lease incentive of $13,500.

Derecognition

At the termination of a lease, the right-of-use asset and associated lease liability are removed from the books. The difference between the two amounts is accounted for as a profit or loss at that time. If the lessee purchases the underlying asset at the termination of a lease, then any difference between the purchase price and the lease liability is recorded as an adjustment to the asset's carrying amount.

Summary

The accounting for leases is an order of magnitude more difficult than for the other types of accounting described in this book, especially in regard to the treatment of a right-of-use asset (which is a recent addition to the accounting standards). One way to deal with the issue is to only use short-term leases, which do not require the recognition of a right-of-use asset. Another alternative is to pursue other financing options when acquiring fixed assets. When all else fails, bring in a lease accounting expert to review the company's entries and verify that they are correct.

Chapter 11
Payroll Accounting

Introduction

One of the primary responsibilities of the accountant in a construction company is to process payroll, since the business may employ a large core group that works on its jobs. This chapter contains the essentials of payroll accounting activities, covering the following topics:

- Employee time tracking
- Gross pay calculations
- Types of payroll taxes
- Income tax withholdings
- Benefits and other deductions
- Net pay
- Remitting payroll taxes
- Payments to employees
- The payroll register
- Payroll journal entries

The ordering of these topics approximates the flow of transactions for the processing of payroll, from the initial collection of time worked information, through the determination of gross pay, and concluding with net pay, payments to employees, and the recordation of payroll.

Related Podcast Episodes: Episodes 126-129 of the Accounting Best Practices Podcast discuss the payroll system. They are available at: **accounting-tools.com/podcasts** or **iTunes**

Employee Time Tracking

In order to pay hourly employees, it is necessary to have a system in place for tracking their hours worked. In a construction environment, this means having fields on a timesheet that allow for the identification of the job, phase and task to which time is being charged. These entries can be relatively complex, so supervisors may fill out this information in order to ensure that the correct job codes are charged and then have employees verify the information. Both the employee and his or her supervisor should sign the card. A sample timesheet appears in the next exhibit.

Sample Timesheet

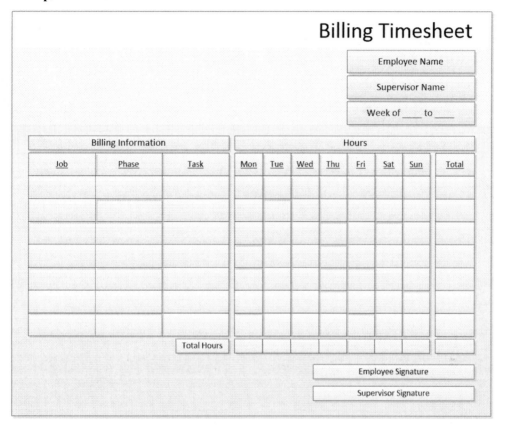

Gross Pay Calculations

Gross pay is the amount of compensation to be paid to an employee before any deductions are withheld from the pay. Though not especially difficult to calculate, there are some issues to consider when deriving gross pay, which are dealt with in the following sub-sections.

Hourly Rate Plan

The simplest and most commonly-used method for determining the compensation of an hourly employee is the hourly rate plan, under which hours worked are multiplied by an employee's hourly rate. This method can be more complicated if there is a shift differential or overtime. A shift differential is extra pay earned by employees who work a less than desirable shift, such as the evening, night, or weekend shifts.

EXAMPLE

Arlo Montaigne works the night shift as a laborer at Montague Construction. He earns a base wage of $13.50 per hour, plus a $0.50 shift differential. In the most recent work week, he logs 39 hours of work. The calculation of his wages earned under the hourly rate plan is:

($13.50 base wage + $0.50 shift differential) × 39 hours = $546.00

If there is a shift differential, add it to the base wage prior to calculating overtime.

What if an employee works a fraction of an hour? A computerized payroll system automatically converts this to a fraction of an hour. However, an accountant that manually calculates wages may use a variety of simplification methods, such as rounding up to the nearest quarter-hour.

EXAMPLE

The Mickelson Construction Company calculates wages for its employees by hand. In the most recent week, Mortimer Davis worked 39 hours and 41 minutes. The company's accountant could use a calculator to determine that 41 minutes is 0.6833 hours (calculated as 41 minutes ÷ 60 minutes) and pay the employee on that basis. However, prior calculation errors have led to a company policy of rounding up to the next quarter hour. Accordingly, the accountant rounds the 41 minutes up to 45 minutes, and therefore records 39 ¾ hours for Mr. Davis.

Overtime

Overtime is a 50% multiplier that is added to an employee's base wage for hours worked over 40 hours in a work week. This calculation is subject to some variation by state, so review local regulations to see if there is an overriding overtime calculation in place. Here are two rules to consider when calculating overtime pay:

- Do not include in the 40 base hours such special hours as holidays, jury duty, sick time, or vacations.
- Add the shift differential (the extra amount paid to someone working a late shift) to the base wage and then calculate overtime based on this combined figure.

EXAMPLE

Alfredo Montoya works the evening shift at a job site, which adds $1 of shift differential per hour to his base wage of $15 per hour. In the most recent work week, he worked 50 hours. The overtime premium he will be paid is based on the combined $16 wage that includes his shift differential. Thus, his overtime rate is $8 per hour. The calculation of his total compensation for that week is:

50 hours × aggregate base pay of $16/hour	=	$800
10 hours × overtime premium of $8/hour	=	80
Total compensation	=	$880

EXAMPLE

Alfredo Montoya works 35 hours during a week that includes Memorial Day. His employer will pay him for a 43-hour work week, which adds the eight hours of the federal holiday to his hours worked. However, this will not include any overtime pay, since only 35 hours were actually worked.

There may be situations where an employee is paid different rates at different times during the work period. This situation may arise when the individual works on different jobs that have differing rates of pay associated with them. In these cases, there are three possible options for calculating overtime, which are:

- Base the overtime rate on the highest wage rate paid during the period
- Base the overtime rate on the average wage rate paid during the period
- Base the overtime rate on the wage rate paid after the 40th hour

The last alternative for calculating overtime requires the prior approval of the affected employee.

EXAMPLE

Marcel Moheko worked on two maintenance jobs at a job site during the past work week. He worked on Job A for 30 hours and was paid $20.00 per hour while working on that job. He worked 15 hours on Job B and was paid $25.00 per hour for that job. The last job on which he worked was Job A. The calculation of his overtime pay under the three calculation methods is:

	Based on Highest Rate	Based on Average Rate	Based on Last Rate
Job A pay rate	$20.00	$20.00	$20.00
Job B pay rate	$25.00	$25.00	$25.00
Weighted average pay rate*	$21.25	$21.25	$21.25
Overtime rate	$12.50	$10.63	$10.00
Overtime hours	5	5	5
Total overtime paid	$62.50	$53.15	$50.00

* Calculated as ($20.00 × 75%) + ($25.00 × 25%)

Types of Payroll Taxes

The government requires employers to pay three types of taxes related to payroll, which are Social Security, Medicare, and unemployment taxes. In the following subsections, we address the nature, amount, and calculation of each tax.

Social Security Tax

The social security tax began with the passage of the Social Security Act in 1935, which established Old Age and Survivor's Insurance. The insurance was to be funded by compulsory deductions from the pay of wage earners. Initially, these deductions were set at 1% of gross wages, were to be paid by both the employer and the employee, and would continue until retirement age, which was set at 65. By 1948, the amount of these deductions had increased to 3%. Employers have been and continue to be responsible for withholding the social security tax from employee pay.

The tax rate for social security is now governed by the Federal Insurance Contributions Act (FICA). Because of this association, social security taxes are now closely associated with the acronym "FICA".

This tax has increased in size over time, along with the maximum wage cap (also known as the *wage base limit*) to which it applies. The social security tax rate is only applied to a person's wages up to the amount of the wage base cap. Do not apply the tax to any wages earned above the wage cap. For example, on earnings of $150,000 in 2016, the amount of employer tax paid would be $7,347.00, which is calculated as follows:

6.2% Tax rate × $118,500 Wage cap = $7,347.00

The following table shows the recent history of the social security tax for the past few years.

Tax Year	FICA Tax Rate	Wage Cap
2016	6.2%	$118,500
2015	6.2%	118,500
2014	6.2%	117,000

Note that social security is matched by the employee, so the total tax amount paid to the government by the employer is 12.4%.

EXAMPLE

Benjamin Mayhew earned $200,000 in 2016. Based on the $118,500 wage cap in place that year, his employer must deduct $7,347.00 from his gross pay and match it with another $7,347.00 for a total payment of $14,694.00.

Medicare Tax

Medicare is a health insurance program that is administered by the United States government, and which is primarily available to those 65 years old or older, as well as to those with certain disabilities. It is funded through the Medicare tax, though participants must also pay a portion of all health insurance costs incurred. The program has been in existence since 1965.

Since 1986, the Medicare tax rate that is paid by an employee has been 1.45% (plus matching of the same amount by the employer). There is no cap on the Medicare tax for employed and self-employed people; thus, everyone must pay it, irrespective of the amount of money that they earn.

As of 2014, an additional Medicare tax of 0.9% was imposed, which applies to all wages earned in excess of $250,000 for married filers and in excess of $200,000 for single and head of household filers.

EXAMPLE

The Armonk Construction Company employs Mr. Smith, who earns $5,000 of gross pay in the most recent pay period. Armonk withholds $72.50 ($5,000 × .0145) from the pay of Mr. Smith, matches the $72.50 from its own funds, and forwards $145.00 to the government.

Unemployment Taxes

The federal and state governments of the United States provide unemployment compensation to workers who have lost their jobs. This compensation is paid for primarily by employers, who pay both federal and state unemployment taxes.

The FUTA tax rate is 6.0%. Calculate the FUTA tax based on only the first $7,000 paid to each employee in the form of wages during the year (i.e., there is no FUTA tax on wages higher than $7,000 in each calendar year). Then subtract a credit from the FUTA tax for the amount of tax paid into the state unemployment tax fund. The maximum (and most common) amount of this credit is 5.4%, which means that the actual amount of FUTA tax is only 0.6%.

EXAMPLE

Paisley Underwater Contractors employs 100 highly skilled deep sea divers, all of whom earn more than $100,000 per year. Thus, they all earn more than the $7,000 FUTA wage cap in the first quarter of the year. Within the first quarter, Paisley has $700,000 of wages eligible for the FUTA tax (calculated as 100 employees × $7,000). Its FUTA tax liability is the 6.0% federal rate minus the 5.4% state rate, multiplied by the $700,000 of eligible wages. Paisley's FUTA tax liability is therefore $4,200 (calculated as $700,000 eligible wages × 0.6%).

FUTA taxes are remitted on a quarterly basis. If the total amount of tax payable is less than $500 in any quarter, the employer can opt to carry the liability forward to the next quarter. The liability can continue to roll forward through additional quarters if the liability remains less than $500.

Each state has its own unemployment insurance program, which evaluates unemployment claims and administers the payment of benefits to individuals. Each of the states has its own rules regarding who is eligible for unemployment benefits, the amounts to be paid, and the duration of those payments, within guidelines set by the federal government.

State governments impose a state-level unemployment tax on employers that can be quite high – even more than the 5.4% credit allowed under FUTA, as noted earlier. A state typically assigns a relatively high default tax rate to a new business and then subsequently adjusts that rate based on the history of unemployment claims made by employees of the business (known as the *experience rating*). If a business rarely lays off its staff, it will eventually be assigned a lower tax rate, with the reverse being true for a business with an uneven employment record.

States mail unemployment rate notices for the upcoming year to businesses near the end of the current calendar year. Include the tax rate noted on the form in the company's payroll calculations for all of the following year.

Income Tax Withholdings

If an individual is classified as an employee, the employer is responsible for withholding income taxes from that person's gross wages. A key input to the calculation of income tax withholdings is the number of exemptions claimed by an individual on his Form W-4. An example of a completed Form W-4 is provided.

The Form W-4 is completed by each employee, preferably every year, and it contains the number of withholding allowances that they want to claim. Each incremental withholding allowance claimed reduces the amount of federal income tax that the employer must withhold from their pay. When employees complete the Form W-4, they have the option of basing their withholding amount on a fixed dollar amount, a percentage of gross wages, or a percentage of gross wages *and* an additional fixed dollar amount. The amounts specified in the form are the responsibility of the employee, not the company.

> **Tip:** Encourage employees to use the Withholding Calculator located at www.irs.gov/individuals to assist in determining the appropriate number of withholding allowances that they should claim on a Form W-4.

Every employee should complete a Form W-4 when hired, but they are not required by law to do so. If a Form W-4 is not received from an employee, withhold income taxes as though the person were single, with zero withholding allowances (which results in the maximum possible income tax withholding).

Form W-4, Employee's Withholding Allowance Certificate

The IRS provides a set of wage bracket tables for income tax withholdings in its Publication 15, Employer's Tax Guide. This publication is available as a PDF download on the www.irs.gov website. The IRS also provides wage bracket tables that show the total amount of the income tax withholding, social security deduction, and Medicare deduction; these tables are published by the IRS in its Publication 15-A, Employer's Supplemental Tax Guide.

The wage bracket tables are designed to be an easy way to derive the correct amount of income tax withholding for people claiming a reasonable number of withholding allowances (up to ten) and at lower wage levels. Each table calculates the proper amount of withholding under a different set of scenarios. Thus, there are separate wage bracket tables that address the following situations:

Payroll Type	Tables within Payroll Type
Daily	Single, Married
Weekly	Single, Married
Biweekly	Single, Married
Monthly	Single, Married

An extract from a combined wage bracket table is shown in the following exhibit, which is taken from the 2015 version of Publication 15-A. The table lists the amount of income tax withholding, social security deduction, and Medicare taxes to be withheld for a married person who is on a biweekly payroll period. The actual table presents information for a much larger range of income and for more withholding allowances.

IRS Combined Wage Bracket Table for a Married Employee (Biweekly Payroll)

Wages are		The number of withholding allowances claimed is					
	But less	0	1	2	3	4	5
At least	than	The amount of income, social security, and Medicare taxes to be withheld is					
1,005	1,025	145.65	130.65	115.65	99.65	84.65	77.65
1,025	1,045	149.18	134.18	119.18	103.18	88.18	79.18
1,045	1,065	153.71	137.71	122.71	106.71	91.71	80.71
1,065	1,085	158.24	141.24	126.24	110.24	95.24	82.24
1,085	1,105	162.77	144.77	129.77	113.77	98.77	83.77
1,105	1,125	167.30	148.30	133.30	117.30	102.30	87.30
1,125	1,145	171.83	151.83	136.83	120.83	105.83	90.83
1,145	1,165	176.36	155.36	140.36	124.36	109.36	94.36
1,165	1,185	180.89	158.89	143.89	127.89	112.89	97.89
1,185	1,205	185.42	162.42	147.42	131.42	116.42	101.42
1,205	1,225	189.95	166.95	150.95	134.95	119.95	104.95

To use the wage bracket method, go to the table that corresponds to the company's payroll period and for the employee's married status (single or married). Within that table, go to the column corresponding to the number of withholding allowances claimed by the employee and drop down that column until you reach the row corresponding to the wages earned by the employee in the pay period. The amount in that cell represents either the amount of income tax to withhold (if using the Publication 15 table) or the entire amount of income tax, social security, and Medicare to withhold (if using the Publication 15-A table).

EXAMPLE

Albert Montaigne works for Mountain Construction. Mr. Montaigne is an hourly production employee of the company, which pays its staff on a biweekly basis. Mr. Montaigne earned $1,180 during the most recent biweekly period. He has claimed four withholding allowances on his Form W-4. According to the preceding extract from the IRS combined wage bracket table, the company should deduct a total of $112.89 from his wages to cover income tax withholdings, as well as social security and Medicare taxes.

Benefits and Other Deductions

Thus far, we have described a set of mandatory deductions from gross pay related to taxes. In addition, there are a number of other deductions that may be taken from gross pay. The essential information related to these deductions is described in the following bullet points:

- *Benefits deductions.* A company that wants to retain its employees over the long term may offer them a benefits package that could include medical, dental, vision, life, short-term and long-term disability insurance. The amount deducted from employee pay is typically the residual amount owed after the company pays for a portion of the underlying expense.
- *Charitable contributions.* Many employers encourage their employees to make contributions to local or national charities, and may also match these contributions to some extent. Under such an arrangement, an employee signs a pledge card, which authorizes the company to deduct certain contribution amounts from their pay on an ongoing basis. The company then periodically forwards the sum total of all contributions deducted to the targeted charities, along with any matching amount that the company is paying.
- *Garnishments.* Some people resist fulfilling their legal obligations to other parties, or they do not have the financial resources to do so. If the company employs such a person, it is quite possible that the accountant will receive a garnishment order, under which the entity must withhold specified amounts from an employee's pay and forward it to a third party. A garnishment order usually relates to child support, unpaid taxes, or unpaid student loans.
- *Union dues.* If a company has entered into a collective bargaining agreement with a labor union, the terms of the agreement usually stipulate that the company withhold union dues from employee pay and forward it to the union.
- *Deductions for financing repayments.* A business may issue advances or loans to its employees. If so, deductions from future paychecks will be needed to reduce the balances of these outstanding amounts.

Net Pay

Net pay is the amount paid to employees after all of the deductions described in the previous sections are deducted from gross pay. The entire net pay calculation may be included in a remittance advice that is forwarded to employees along with their paychecks. A typical calculation format that may be given to an employee is as follows:

Gross pay (40 hours × $30.00/hour)	$1,200.00
Deductions:	
Social security	74.40
Medicare	17.40
Income tax withholding	225.00
Medical insurance	160.00
Union dues	15.00
Garnishments	100.00
Net pay	$608.20

Remitting Payroll Taxes

An employer has a legal obligation to forward to the government all income taxes that it has withheld from employee pay, as well as social security and Medicare taxes. These remittances must be forwarded to the government in accordance with a specific payment schedule and method that is described in the following sub-sections. In this section, we review when tax deposits should be made, how to remit funds, and related reporting requirements.

If an employer were to miss a timely remittance, or pay an insufficient amount, the related penalty would be severe. For this reason alone, it is important to have a detailed understanding of tax remittances.

Types of Tax Deposit Schedules

There are two deposit schedules, known as the *monthly deposit schedule* and the *semiweekly deposit schedule* that state when to deposit payroll taxes. You must determine which of these deposit schedules will be followed before the beginning of each calendar year. The selection of a deposit schedule is based entirely on the tax liability reported during a *lookback period.*

The deposit schedule is based on the total taxes (i.e., federal income taxes withheld, social security taxes, and Medicare taxes) reported in line 8 of the Forms 941 in a four-quarter lookback period. The lookback period begins on July 1 and ends on June 30. The decision tree for selecting a deposit period is:

- If the business reported $50,000 or less of taxes during the lookback period, use the monthly deposit schedule.
- If the business reported more than $50,000 of taxes during the lookback period, use the semiweekly deposit schedule.

> **Note:** Do not select a deposit schedule based on how often the company pays employees or makes deposits. It is solely based on the total tax liability reported during the lookback period.

EXAMPLE

Selective Construction Company had used the monthly deposit schedule in previous years, but its payroll expanded considerably in the past year, which may place it in the semiweekly deposit schedule. Selective's accountant calculates the amount of taxes paid during its lookback period to see if the semiweekly deposit schedule now applies. The calculation is:

Lookback Period	Taxes Paid
July 1 – September 30, 2015	$8,250
October 1 – December 31, 2015	14,750
January 1 – March 31, 2016	17,500
April 1 – June 30, 2016	19,000
Total	$59,500

Since the total amount of taxes that Selective paid during the lookback period exceeded $50,000, the company must use the semiweekly deposit schedule during the next calendar year.

> **Tip:** A new employer has no lookback period, and so is automatically considered a monthly schedule depositor for its first calendar year of business.

The schedule for depositing state withholding taxes varies by state. Consult with the applicable state government for this deposit schedule. If the business outsources payroll processing, the supplier will handle these deposits on the organization's behalf.

Monthly Deposit Schedule

If a business qualifies to use the monthly deposit schedule, deposit employment taxes on payments made during a month by the 15th day of the following month.

EXAMPLE

Jiffy Construction is a monthly schedule depositor that pays its staff on the 15th and last business day of each month. Under the monthly deposit schedule, Jiffy must deposit the combined tax liabilities for all of its payrolls in a month by the 15th day of the following month. The same deposit schedule would apply if Jiffy had instead paid its employees every day, every other week, twice a month, once a month, or on any other payroll schedule.

The total payroll taxes withheld for each of Jiffy's payrolls in September are noted in the following table, along with the amount of its tax liability that will be due for remittance to the government on October 15:

	Federal Income Tax Withheld	Social Security Tax Withheld	Medicare Tax Withheld
Sept. 15 payroll	$1,500.00	$620.00	$145.00
Sept. 30 payroll	1,250.00	558.00	130.50
Sept. total withheld	$2,750.00	$1,178.00	$275.50
Employer tax matching	--	1,178.00	275.50
Tax deposit due Oct. 15	$2,750.00	$2,356.00	$551.00

Jiffy's tax liability to be remitted on October 15 is $5,657.00, which is calculated as the total of all withholdings and employer matches for federal income taxes, social security taxes, and Medicare taxes ($2,750.00 + $2,356.00 + $551.00).

Semiweekly Deposit Schedule

If an employer qualifies to use the semiweekly deposit schedule, remit payroll taxes using the following table:

Payment Date	Corresponding Deposit Date
Wednesday, Thursday, or Friday	Following Wednesday
Saturday, Sunday, Monday, Tuesday	Following Friday

If an employer has more than one pay date during a semiweekly period and the pay dates fall in different calendar quarters, make separate deposits for the liabilities associated with each pay date.

EXAMPLE

Lincoln Log Construction has a pay date on Wednesday, June 29 (second quarter) and another pay date on Friday, July 1 (third quarter). Lincoln must make a separate deposit for the taxes associated with each pay date, even though both dates fall within the same semiweekly period. The company should pay both deposits on the following Wednesday, July 6.

EXAMPLE

Rustic Cabin Contractors uses the semiweekly deposit schedule. The company only pays its employees once a month, on the last day of the month. Although Rustic is on a semiweekly deposit schedule, it can only make a deposit once a month, since it only pays its employees once a month.

Note that the semiweekly deposit method does not mean that an employer is required to make two tax deposits per week – it is simply the name of the method. Thus, if a company has one payroll every other week, it would remit taxes only every other week.

The differentiating factor between the monthly and semiweekly deposit schedules is that an employer must remit taxes much more quickly under the semiweekly method. The monthly method uses a simpler and more delayed tax deposit schedule, which is ideal for smaller businesses.

Federal Unemployment Deposit Schedule

The federal unemployment tax is to be deposited on a quarterly basis. The deposit dates are:

Relevant Calendar Quarter	Last Possible Deposit Date
First quarter of the calendar year	April 30
Second quarter of the calendar year	July 31
Third quarter of the calendar year	October 31
Fourth quarter of the calendar year	January 31

Remittance Method

All federal tax deposits must be paid by electronic funds transfer. Use the Electronic Federal Tax Payment System (EFTPS) to make these deposits. EFTPS is a free service that is maintained by the Department of Treasury. The system can either be used directly or through an intermediary, such as the company's payroll supplier (if the business is outsourcing payroll) to deposit the funds on the company's behalf. Go to www.eftps.gov to enroll in EFTPS. If the business is a new employer, it will likely have been pre-enrolled in EFTPS when it applied for an employer identification number (EIN); if so, the company will receive a personal identification number for the EFTPS system as part of the initial EIN package of information.

When remitting taxes to the government, the remittance should include the following types of taxes:
- Withheld income taxes
- Withheld and matching employer social security taxes
- Withheld and matching employer Medicare taxes

When a deposit is made, EFTPS will provide a deposit trace number, which can be used as a receipt or to trace the payment.

The Form 941 Quarterly Federal Tax Return

Following each calendar quarter, any employer that pays wages subject to income tax withholding, or social security and Medicare taxes, must file a Form 941, the Employer's Quarterly Federal Tax Return. The Form 941 must be filed by the last day of the month following the calendar quarter to which it applies. Thus, the filing dates for the Form 941 are:

Quarter Ending	Form 941 Due Date
March 31	April 30
June 30	July 31
September 30	October 31
December 31	January 31

If a Form 941 is not filed in a timely manner (not including filing extensions), the IRS imposes a failure-to-file penalty of 5% of the unpaid tax due with that return, up to a maximum penalty of 25% of the tax due. In addition, for each whole month or part of a month that payment is late, there is an additional failure-to-pay penalty of ½% of the amount of the tax, up to a maximum of 25% of the tax due. If both penalties apply in a month, the failure-to-file penalty is reduced by the amount of the failure-to-pay penalty. The IRS may waive these penalties if a reasonable cause can be presented for failing to file the Form 941 or pay the tax due.

State Tax Remittances

Each state government has its own system for reporting and depositing state-level payroll taxes. The types of taxes can vary from those collected at the federal level and may include the following: ,

- State income tax
- Unemployment insurance tax
- Disability insurance tax
- Special district taxes (such as for a transportation district)

The forms used to report this information vary by state. The primary reports that may be required are:

- *Reconciliation statement.* Compares the amount of state taxes remitted to the amount withheld from employee pay.
- *Tax withholdings.* Reports wages paid to employees and the state taxes withheld from their pay.

Most state governments provide preprinted tax remittance and reporting forms to those employers registered to do business within their boundaries. If an employer outsources its payroll, the supplier is responsible for completing and submitting these forms.

The required remittance dates also vary by state, as do the modes of payment – either check or electronic payments may be required. In some cases, an employer can choose between modes of payment, though it is customary to require electronic payment for all future payments, once an employer has switched to that type of payment.

Each state government publishes an explanatory guide to its tax structure, in which it describes the state's reporting and remittance system. These guides are usually also available online as PDF documents or web pages.

Payments to Employees

The standard method for paying employees for many years was the check, though it has been largely supplanted by direct deposit. A check is usually accompanied by a *remittance advice* (also known as a *check stub*), on which is listed an employee's gross pay, tax deductions and other withholdings, and net pay. A simplified sample remittance advice for a one-week pay period is:

Employee Name: Arturo Johansson							[company name]
Ending Pay Date	Hours Worked	Rate	Gross Pay	Federal Inc. Tax	Social Security	Medicare	Net Pay
5/15/xx	Regular 40 OT 10	$20.00 $30.00	$1,100.00	$197.25	$68.20	$15.95	$818.60

Direct deposit involves the electronic transfer of funds from the company to the bank accounts of its employees, using the Automated Clearing House (ACH) system. ACH is an electronic network for the processing of both debit and credit transactions within the United States and Canada.

The payment process is to calculate pay in the same manner as for check payments, but to then send the payment information to a direct deposit processing service, which initiates electronic payments to the bank accounts of those employees being paid in this manner. The processing service deducts the funds from a company bank account in advance of the direct deposits, so cash flow tends to be somewhat more accelerated than is the case if a company were to issue checks and then wait several days for the amounts on the checks to be withdrawn from its bank account.

Direct deposit is more efficient than payments by check, because it does not require a signature on each payment, there are no checks to be delivered, and employees do not have to waste time depositing them at a bank. Further, employees working at construction sites can still rely upon having cash paid into their accounts in a timely manner.

Direct deposit can also be more efficient from the perspective of the remittance advice. A number of payroll suppliers offer an option to simply notify employees by e-mail when their pay has been sent to them, after which employees can access a secure website to view their remittance advice information. This approach is better than sending a paper version of a remittance advice, because employees can also access many years of historical pay information on-line, as well as their W-2 forms.

The implementation of direct deposit can cause some initial difficulties, because each person's bank account information must be correctly set up in the direct deposit module of the company's payroll software (or software provided by the outsourced payroll supplier). This initial setup is remarkably prone to error, and also usually requires a test transaction (the *pre-notification*) that delays implementation by one pay period. Consequently, even if a new employee signs up for direct deposit immediately, the accountant must still print a paycheck for that person's first payroll, after which direct deposit can be used.

> **Tip:** If employees want to be paid by direct deposit, require them to submit a voided check for the checking account into which they want funds to be sent. You can more reliably take the routing and account numbers directly from such a check, rather than risking a transposition error if an employee copies this information onto a form. Also, do not accept a deposit slip instead of a check – the information on the deposit slip may not match the routing and account number information on the check.

A final issue with direct deposit is being able to do so from an in-house payroll processing function. If the payroll software does not provide for direct deposit, it will be necessary to contract with a third party to make the payments on behalf of the company. Direct deposit is much easier to implement if the company is outsourcing payroll, since direct deposit is part of the standard feature set for all payroll suppliers.

The Payroll Register

The primary internal report generated by the payroll system is the payroll register. This document itemizes the calculation of wages, taxes, and deductions for each employee for each payroll. There are multiple uses for the payroll register, including:

- *Investigation.* It is the starting point for the investigation of many issues involving employee pay.
- *Journal entries.* Journal entries are created to record a payroll based on the information in the register.
- *Payments.* If manual check payments are being created, the source document for these payments is the register.
- *Reports.* The information on almost any government or management report related to payroll is drawn from the register.

The format of the payroll register is built into the payroll software and so will vary somewhat by payroll system. If payroll processing is outsourced, the supplier will issue its own version of the payroll register as part of its basic service package. The following is a typical payroll register format, with overtime and state and local taxes removed in order to compress the presentation:

Sample Payroll Register

Empl. Nbr.	Employee Name	Hours Worked	Rate/ Hour	Gross Wages	Taxes	Other Deductions	Check Nbr.	Net Pay
100	Johnson, Mark	40	18.12	724.80	55.45	28.00	5403	641.35
105	Olds, Gary	27	36.25	978.75	74.87	42.25	5404	861.63
107	Zeff, Morton	40	24.00	960.00	73.44	83.00	5405	803.56
111	Quill, Davis	40	15.00	600.00	45.90	10.10	5406	544.00
116	Pincus, Joseph	35	27.75	971.25	74.30	37.50	5407	859.45

A comprehensive payroll register will include the following fields:

- *Employee number*. This is a unique identification number for each employee. The preceding report is sorted by employee number.
- *Department number*. In larger organizations, it is an excellent idea to assign a department number to each employee, so that departmental wage information can be more easily aggregated and charged to the correct department.
- *Employee name*. This is usually presented in last name, first name format. The payroll register may be sorted by employee last name, rather than by employee number.
- *Salary/wage indicator*. There may be a flag in the report that indicates whether an employee is paid a fixed salary or an hourly wage.
- *Marriage code*. This is a flag in the report, indicating whether a person is classified as married or single. Marriage status impacts the amount of income taxes withheld.
- *Allowances number*. This is the number of allowances that a person has claimed on his or her Form W-4. The number of allowances is used to calculate the amount of income taxes withheld.
- *Total hours worked*. This is the combined total of regular and overtime hours worked, and should tie back to the hours listed in the timekeeping system.
- *Regular hours worked*. This states the total amount of regular hours worked during the payroll period, and is used to calculate gross pay.
- *Overtime hours worked*. This states the total amount of overtime hours worked during the payroll period, and is used to calculate gross pay.
- *Regular hours pay rate*. This rate is multiplied by regular hours worked to arrive at part of the gross pay figure.
- *Overtime hours pay rate*. This rate is multiplied by overtime hours worked to arrive at part of the gross pay figure.
- *Gross pay*. This combines wages paid from regular and overtime hours worked and is the grand total from which deductions are then made to arrive at net pay.
- *Federal income tax withholding*. This is the federal-level income taxes withheld from employee gross wages.

- *Social security tax.* This is the employee-paid portion of the social security tax. It does not include the employer-matched amount of the tax.
- *Medicare tax.* This is the employee-paid portion of the Medicare tax. It does not include the employer-matched amount of the tax.
- *State income tax withholding.* This is the state income taxes withheld from employee wages.
- *Other deductions.* This can include a broad array of deductions, such as for medical insurance, life insurance, pension plan contributions, and so forth. Identify each type of deduction on the report with a unique code. Thus, deductions for medical insurance could be identified with the MED code, while deductions for life insurance could be identified with the LIFE code.
- *Net pay.* This is the amount of cash paid to each employee after all deductions have been made from gross pay.
- *Check number.* This is the unique identifying number listed on each paycheck issued, and is used by the bank to identify cleared checks (among other uses).
- *Payment type.* This is a code that states whether payment was made with a check, direct deposit, or debit card.

Tip: Do *not* include employee social security numbers in the payroll register, since these reports may end up in the wrong hands, leading to inappropriate dissemination of the social security numbers.

The payroll register should also provide a variety of summary-level information that can be used to record wage and tax information in the general ledger. It should aggregate gross wages, each type of deduction, state-level taxes withheld by individual state, and the total amount of cash paid. If you report at the department level, the payroll register should provide this information not only in total for the entire company, but also at the department level.

If a company were to create a payroll register that contained all of the items in the preceding list, it would be an exceptionally crowded report. However, packing information into the payroll register makes it a great source document when researching payroll issues. Consequently, it is better to create a near-comprehensive payroll register format, rather than one containing the minimum amount of information.

Form W-2

Following the end of every calendar year, and no later than January 31, an employer must issue the multi-part Form W-2, on which it itemizes the wages it paid to each employee during the year, as well as the taxes that it withheld from employee pay. It issues this form to anyone who was paid wages by the company at any time during the year, even if they no longer work for the business. This information forms the basis for the personal income tax returns completed by all employees for the federal government and the state government in which they reside. An example of the Form W-2 is shown next.

Sample Form W-2

The Form W-2 contains a large number of fields, but many of them are not needed to report the compensation and tax information for a typical employee; many of the fields are only required to report unusual compensation arrangements. The payroll system prints these forms automatically after the end of the calendar year. If the organization is outsourcing payroll, the supplier will issue them on the company's behalf. Thus, the Form W-2 is usually not an especially difficult document to produce.

Payroll Journal Entries

The payroll system may be entirely separate from a company's primary system of recording accounting transactions. This is especially true if it has outsourced the payroll function entirely. Thus, the accountant will need a process for transferring the information accumulated in the payroll system to the accounting system. The chief tool for doing so is the journal entry. This section describes where payroll information is stored in an accounting system and the journal entries used to record payroll information in that system.

Note: The accounting system does not contain information about employee-specific wage and benefit information. The payroll system must be accessed to obtain this information.

142

Types of Payroll Journal Entries

There are several types of journal entries that involve the recordation of compensation. The primary entry is for the initial recordation of a payroll. This entry records the gross wages earned by employees, as well as all withholdings from their pay and any additional taxes owed by the company. There may also be an accrued wages entry that is recorded at the end of each accounting period, which is intended to record the amount of wages owed to employees but not yet paid. These types of compensation are based on different source documents and require separate calculations and journal entries. There are also a number of other payroll-related journal entries that a payroll staff must deal with on a regular basis. They include:

- Manual paychecks
- Employee advances
- Accrued vacation pay
- Tax deposits

All of these journal entries are described in the following sub-sections.

Primary Payroll Journal Entry

The primary journal entry for payroll is the summary-level entry that is compiled from the payroll register. This entry usually includes debits for the direct labor expense, wages, and the company's portion of payroll taxes. There will also be credits to a number of other accounts, each one detailing the liability for payroll taxes that have not been paid, as well as for the amount of cash already paid to employees for their net pay. The basic entry (assuming no further breakdown of debits by individual department) is:

	Debit	Credit
Wages expense [expense account]	xxx	
Payroll taxes expense [expense account]	xxx	
Cash [asset account]		xxx
Federal withholding taxes payable [liability account]		xxx
Social security taxes payable [liability account]		xxx
Medicare taxes payable [liability account]		xxx
Federal unemployment taxes payable [liability account]		xxx
State unemployment taxes payable [liability account]		xxx
Garnishments payable [liability account]		xxx

When an employee charges a job on his time sheet, the accounting staff will charge the cost of those hours to the relevant job, phase, and cost code in the job cost ledger. The job type code will be "L," to classify this expenditure as labor. Those wage expenses charged to jobs will then appear in the cost of construction – labor account.

> **Note:** The reason for the payroll taxes expense line item in this journal entry is that the company incurs the cost of matching the social security and Medicare amounts paid by employees and directly incurs the cost of unemployment insurance. The employee-paid portions of the social security and Medicare taxes are not recorded as expenses; instead, they are liabilities for which the company has an obligation to remit cash to the taxing government entity.

A key point with this journal entry is that the wages expense contains employee gross pay, while the amount actually paid to employees through the cash account is their net pay. The difference between the two figures (which can be substantial) is the amount of deductions from their pay, such as payroll taxes and withholdings to pay for benefits.

There may be a number of additional employee deductions to include in this journal entry. For example, there may be deductions for 401(k) pension plans, health insurance, life insurance, vision insurance, and for the repayment of advances.

When the company later pays the withheld taxes and company portion of payroll taxes, use the following entry to reduce the balance in the cash account and eliminate the balances in the liability accounts:

	Debit	Credit
Federal withholding taxes payable [liability account]	xxx	
Social security taxes payable [liability account]	xxx	
Medicare taxes payable [liability account]	xxx	
Federal unemployment taxes payable [liability account]	xxx	
State withholding taxes payable [liability account]	xxx	
State unemployment taxes payable [liability account]	xxx	
Garnishments payable [liability account]	xxx	
Cash [asset account]		xxx

Thus, when a company initially deducts taxes and other items from an employee's pay, the company incurs a liability to pay the taxes to a third party. This liability only disappears from the company's accounting records when it pays the related funds to the entity to which they are owed.

Accrued Wages

It is quite common to have some amount of unpaid wages at the end of an accounting period, so accrue this expense (if it is material). The accrual entry, as shown next, is simpler than the comprehensive payroll entry already shown, because all payroll taxes are typically clumped into a single expense account and offsetting liability account. This entry is *not* charged to specific jobs, since it is only designed to ensure that the correct aggregate wage expense is recorded within the reporting period. After recording this entry, reverse it at the beginning of the following accounting period, and then record the actual payroll expense whenever it occurs.

	Debit	Credit
Wages expense [expense account]	xxx	
Accrued salaries and wages [liability account]		xxx
Accrued payroll taxes [liability account]		xxx

The information for the wage accrual entry is most easily derived from a spreadsheet that itemizes all employees to whom the calculation applies, the amount of unpaid time, and the standard pay rate for each person. It is not necessary to also calculate the cost of overtime hours earned during an accrual period if the amount of such hours is relatively small. A sample spreadsheet for calculating accrued wages is:

Hourly Employees	Unpaid Days	Hourly Rate	Pay Accrual
Anthem, Jill	4	$20.00	$640
Bingley, Adam	4	18.25	584
Chesterton, Elvis	4	17.50	560
Davis, Ethel	4	23.00	736
Ellings, Humphrey	4	21.50	688
Fogarty, Miriam	4	16.00	512
		Total	$3,720

Manual Paycheck Entry

It is all too common to create a manual paycheck, either because an employee was short-paid in a prior payroll or because the company is laying off or firing an employee and so is obligated to pay that person before the next regularly scheduled payroll. This check may be paid through the corporate accounts payable bank account, rather than its payroll account, so it may be necessary to make this entry through the accounts payable system.

EXAMPLE

The Aspen Grove Construction Company lays off Mr. Jones. Aspen Grove owes Mr. Jones $5,000 of wages at the time of the layoff. The accountant calculates that Aspen Grove must withhold $382.50 from Mr. Jones' pay to cover the employee-paid portions of social security and Medicare taxes. Mr. Jones has claimed a large enough number of withholding allowances that there is no income tax withholding. Thus, the company pays Mr. Jones $4,617.50. The journal entry it uses is:

	Debit	Credit
Wage expense	5,000.00	
Social security taxes payable		310.00
Medicare taxes payable		72.50
Cash		4,617.50

At the next regularly-scheduled payroll, the accountant records this payment as a notation in the payroll system, so that it will properly compile the correct amount of wages for Mr. Jones for his year-end Form W-2. In addition, the payroll system calculates that Aspen Grove must pay a matching amount of social security and Medicare taxes (though no unemployment taxes, since Mr. Jones already exceeded his wage cap for these taxes). Accordingly, an additional liability of $382.50 is recorded in the payroll journal entry for that payroll. Aspen Grove pays these matching amounts as part of its normal tax remittances associated with the payroll.

Employee Advances

When an employee asks for an advance, this is recorded as a current asset in the company's balance sheet. There may not be a separate account in which to store advances, especially if employee advances are infrequent; possible asset accounts that can be used are:
- Employee advances (for high-volume situations)
- Other assets (probably sufficient for smaller construction companies that record few assets other than trade receivables, inventory, and fixed assets)
- Other receivables (useful if the accountant is tracking a number of different types of assets, and wants to segregate receivables in one account)

EXAMPLE

Blank Wall Construction issues a $1,000 advance to employee Wes Smith. Blank Wall issues advances regularly, and so uses a separate account in which to record advances. It records the transaction as:

	Debit	Credit
Other assets	1,000	
Cash		1,000

One week later, Mr. Smith pays back half the amount of the advance, which is recorded with this entry:

	Debit	Credit
Cash	500	
Other assets		500

No matter what method is later used to repay the company – a check from the employee, or payroll deductions – the entry will be a credit to whichever asset account was used, until such time as the balance in the account has been paid off.

Employee advances require vigilance by the accountant, because employees who have limited financial resources will tend to use the company as their personal banks and so will be reluctant to pay back advances unless pressed repeatedly. Thus, it is essential to continually monitor the remaining amount of advances outstanding for every employee.

Accrued Vacation Pay

Accrued vacation pay is the amount of vacation time that an employee has earned as per a company's employee benefit manual, but which he has not yet used. The calculation of accrued vacation pay for each employee is:

1. Calculate the amount of vacation time earned through the beginning of the accounting period. This should be a roll-forward balance from the preceding period.
2. Add the number of hours earned in the current accounting period.
3. Subtract the number of vacation hours used in the current period.
4. Multiply the ending number of accrued vacation hours by the employee's hourly wage to arrive at the correct accrual that should be on the company's books.
5. If the amount already accrued for the employee from the preceding period is lower than the correct accrual, record the difference as an addition to the accrued liability. If the amount already accrued from the preceding period is higher than the correct accrual, record the difference as a reduction of the accrued liability.

Payroll Accounting

A sample spreadsheet follows that uses the preceding steps, and which can be used to compile accrued vacation pay:

Name	Vacation Roll-Forward Balance	+ New Hours Earned	- Hours Used	= Net Balance	× Hourly Pay	= Accrued Vacation $
Hilton, David	24.0	10	34.0	0.0	$25.00	$0.00
Idle, John	13.5	10	0.0	23.5	17.50	411.25
Jakes, Jill	120.0	10	80.0	50.0	23.50	1,175.00
Kilo, Steve	114.5	10	14.0	110.5	40.00	4,420.00
Linder, Alice	12.0	10	0.0	22.0	15.75	346.50
Mills, Jeffery	83.5	10	65.00	28.5	19.75	562.88
					Total	$6,915.63

It is not necessary to reverse the vacation pay accrual in each period if you choose to instead record just incremental changes in the accrual from month to month.

EXAMPLE

There is already an existing accrued balance of 40 hours of unused vacation time for Wes Smith on the books of Square Corner Construction. In the most recent month that has just ended, Mr. Smith accrued an additional five hours of vacation time (since he is entitled to 60 hours of accrued vacation time per year, and 60 ÷ 12 = five hours per month). He also used three hours of vacation time during the month. This means that, as of the end of the month, Square Corner should have accrued a total of 42 hours of vacation time for him (calculated as 40 hours existing balance + 5 hours additional accrual – 3 hours used).

Mr. Smith is paid $30 per hour, so his total vacation accrual should be $1,260 (42 hours × $30/hour), so Square Corner accrues an additional $60 of vacation liability.

What if an employee receives a pay raise? Then it will be necessary to increase the amount of his entire vacation accrual by the incremental amount of the pay raise. This is because, if the employee were to leave the company and be paid all of his unused vacation pay, he would be paid at his most recent rate of pay.

148

Tax Deposits

When an employer withholds taxes from employee pay, it must deposit these funds with the government at stated intervals. The journal entry for doing so is a debit to the tax liability account being paid and a credit to the cash account, which reduces the cash balance. For example, if a company were to pay a state government for unemployment taxes, the entry would be:

	Debit	Credit
State unemployment taxes payable [liability account]	xxx	
Cash [asset account]		xxx

Summary

The payroll function is one of the most crucial accounting operations, since employees are depending on the accountant to correctly determine gross pay, deductions, and net pay – every time. If a construction company has a continuing problem with payments to employees, this can trigger significant employee dissatisfaction. There are several ways to mitigate payroll errors, which include the following:

- Upgrade the timekeeping system from timecards to an electronic or Internet-based time clock, so that employee hours worked are automatically recorded in the payroll software.
- Outsource payroll processing to a third party. By doing so, a specialist is now being involved in payroll calculations, taxes remittances, and payments to employees. This does not completely eliminate errors, since the accountant must still input information into the third party's system – but errors should decline.
- Use formal procedures as part of every payroll processing activity. Doing so reduces the risk that steps will be missed or completed incorrectly. This is especially important when the accountant is new to payroll processing.

Chapter 12
Investments in Construction Joint Ventures

Introduction

As noted in the introductory chapter, contractors may combine their resources into joint ventures so that they can bid on larger jobs that would otherwise be beyond their reach. There are many types of legal forms that can be used for a construction joint venture, such as general and limited partnerships, limited liability companies, and corporations (see the Business Structures chapter). No matter which legal form is used, the contractor must deal with the accounting for this investment in another entity. In this chapter, we focus primarily on the use of the equity method to do so, as well as the cost method and consolidation accounting.

The Equity Method

When a contractor owns an interest in another business that it does not control (such as a corporate joint venture), it may use the equity method to account for its ownership interest. The equity method is designed to measure changes in the economic results of the investee, by requiring the investor to recognize its share of the profits or losses recorded by the investee. The equity method is a more complex technique of accounting for ownership, and so is typically used only when there is a significant ownership interest that enables an investor to have influence over the decision-making of the investee.

The key determining factor in the use of the equity method is having significant influence over the operating and financial decisions of the investee. The primary determinant of this level of control is owning at least 20% of the voting shares of the investee, though this measurement can be repudiated by evidence that the investee opposes the influence of the investor. Other types of evidence of significant influence are controlling a seat on the board of directors, active participation in the decisions of the investee, or swapping management personnel with the investee.

The investor can avoid using the equity method if it cannot obtain the financial information it needs from the investee in order to correctly account for its ownership interest under the equity method.

The essential accounting under the equity method is for the investor to initially recognize an investment in an investee at cost and then adjust the carrying amount of the investment by recognizing its share of the earnings or losses of the investee in earnings over time. The following additional guidance applies to these basic points:

- *Dividends*. The investor should subtract any dividends received from the investee from the carrying amount of the investor's investment in the investee.

- *Investee losses.* It is possible that the investor's share of the losses of an investee will exceed the carrying amount of its investment in the investee. If so, the investor should report losses up to its carrying amount, as well as any additional financial support given to the investee and then discontinue use of the equity method. However, additional losses can be recorded if it appears assured that the investee will shortly return to profitability. If there is a return to profitability, the investor can return to the equity method only after its share of the profits has been offset by those losses not recognized when use of the equity method was halted.

- *Other write-downs.* If an investor's investment in an investee has been written down to zero, but it has other investments in the investee, the investor should continue to report its share of any additional investee losses, and offset them against the other investments, in sequence of the seniority of those investments (with offsets against the most junior items first). If the investee generates income at a later date, the investor should apply its share of these profits to the other investments in order, with application going against the most senior items first.

- *Ownership increase.* If an investor increases its ownership in an investee, this may qualify it to use the equity method, in which case the investor should retroactively adjust its financial statements for all periods presented to show the investment as though the equity method had been used through the entire reporting period.

- *Ownership decrease.* If an investor decreases its ownership in an investee, this may drop its level of control below the 20% to 25% threshold, in which case the investor may no longer be qualified to use the equity method. If so, the investor should retain the carrying amount of the investment as of the date when the equity method no longer applies, so there is no retroactive adjustment.

EXAMPLE

Armadillo Industries purchases 30% of the common stock of Titanium Contractors, Inc. Armadillo controls two seats on the board of directors of Titanium as a result of this investment, so it has significant influence over Titanium. For this reason, Armadillo uses the equity method to account for the investment. In the next year, Titanium earns $400,000. Armadillo records its 30% share of the profit with the following entry:

	Debit	Credit
Investment in Titanium Contractors	120,000	
Equity in Titanium Contractors income		120,000

A few months later, Titanium issues a $50,000 cash dividend to Armadillo, which the company records with the following entry:

	Debit	Credit
Cash	50,000	
Investment in Titanium Contractors		50,000

EXAMPLE

Armadillo Industries has a 35% ownership interest in the common stock of Arlington Construction. The carrying amount of this investment has been reduced to zero because of previous losses. To keep Arlington solvent, Armadillo has purchased $250,000 of Arlington's preferred stock and extended a long-term unsecured loan of $500,000.

During the next year, Arlington incurs a $1,200,000 loss, of which Armadillo's share is 35%, or $420,000. Since the next most senior level of Arlington's capital after common stock is its preferred stock, Armadillo first offsets its share of the loss against its preferred stock investment. Doing so reduces the carrying amount of the preferred stock to zero, leaving $170,000 to be applied against the carrying amount of the loan. This results in the following entry by Armadillo:

	Debit	Credit
Equity method loss	420,000	
Preferred stock investment		250,000
Loan		170,000

In the following year, Arlington records $800,000 of profits, of which Armadillo's share is $280,000. Armadillo applies the $280,000 first against the loan write-down and then against the preferred stock write-down with the following entry:

	Debit	Credit
Preferred stock investment	110,000	
Loan	170,000	
Equity method income		280,000

The result is that the carrying amount of the loan is fully restored, while the carrying amount of the preferred stock investment is still reduced by $140,000 from its original level.

The Cost Method

What about situations in which a contractor makes a smaller investment in a joint venture that does *not* give it significant influence over the venture? In this case, the firm can use the cost method to account for its ownership interest.

The cost method mandates that the investor account for the investment at its historical cost (i.e., the purchase price). This information appears as an asset on the balance sheet of the investor. Once the investor records the initial transaction, there is no need to adjust it, unless there is evidence that the fair market value of the investment has declined to below the recorded historical cost. If so, the investor writes down the recorded cost of the investment to its new fair market value.

The following accounting rules also apply to the cost method of accounting for investments:

- If the investee pays dividends, the investor records them as dividend income; there is no impact on the investment account.
- If the investee has undistributed earnings, they do not appear in any way in the records of the investor.

EXAMPLE

Hodgson Construction acquires a 10% interest in Eskimo Bidding Corporation for $1,000,000. In the most recent reporting period, Eskimo recognizes $100,000 of net income and issues dividends of $20,000. Under the requirements of the cost method, Hodgson records its initial investment of $1,000,000 and its 10% share of the $20,000 in dividends. Hodgson does not make any other entries.

Consolidations

What about situations in which a contractor owns a majority stake in a joint venture? In this case, the contractor consolidates its financial results with those of the joint venture.

Consolidation accounting is the process of combining the financial results of a contractor and its joint ventures. Consolidated financial statements require considerable effort to construct, since they must exclude the impact of any transactions between the entities being reported on. Thus, if there is a sale of materials between the parent entity and a joint venture, this intercompany sale must be eliminated from the consolidated financial statements. Another common intercompany elimination is when the parent entity pays interest income to the joint venture whose cash it is using to make investments; this interest income must be eliminated from the consolidated financial statements. The following steps document the consolidation accounting process flow:

1. *Record intercompany loans.* If the parent entity has been consolidating the cash balances of its joint ventures into an investment account, record inter-company loans from the joint ventures to the parent entity. Also record an interest income allocation for the interest earned on consolidated invest-ments from the parent entity down to the joint ventures.

2. *Eliminate intercompany transactions.* If there have been any intercompany transactions, reverse them at the parent entity level to eliminate their effects from the consolidated financial statements. Examples of intercompany transactions are:
    - Security holdings
    - Debt
    - Sales (with the reversal of related inventory amounts)
    - Purchases (with the reversal of related inventory amounts)
    - Interest
    - Dividends
    - Gains or losses on asset sales
3. *Eliminate joint venture retained earnings.* Remove the retained earnings of each joint venture as of its acquisition date from the consolidated financial statements.
4. *Defer taxes on inter-company profits.* If income taxes have already been paid on inter-company profits, defer them in the consolidated financial statements. An alternative treatment is to reduce the amount of the inter-entity profits to be eliminated by the amount of the taxes.
5. *Close joint venture books.* Depending upon the accounting software in use, it may be necessary to access the financial records of each joint venture and flag them as closed. This prevents any additional transactions from being recorded in the accounting period being closed.
6. *Close parent entity books.* Flag the parent entity accounting period as closed, so that no additional transactions can be reported in the accounting period being closed.
7. *Issue financial statements.* Print and distribute the consolidated financial statements.

There will be a noncontrolling interest in a joint venture, since there are other owners. This interest is reported in the contractor's consolidated balance sheet as part of equity, but separate from the equity of the contractor. The noncontrolling interest should be clearly labeled as such. The following sample presentation illustrates the concept.

154

Sample Equity Layout within the Balance Sheet

Equity:	
Hilltop Construction shareholders' equity	
Capital stock, $0.01 par	$10,000
Additional paid-in capital	400,000
Retained earnings	2,312,000
Total Hilltop shareholders' equity	$2,722,000
Noncontrolling interest	400,000
Total equity	$3,122,000

If there is a noncontrolling interest in a joint venture, the amount of consolidated net income reported in the income statement should be separated into the amount attributable to the noncontrolling interest and the shareholders of the contractor. The following sample layout illustrates the concept.

Sample Net Income Layout within the Income Statement

Revenues	$10,000,000
Expenses	8,000,000
Net income	2,000,000
Less: Net income attributable to the noncontrolling interest	-400,000
Net income attributable to Hilltop shareholders	$1,600,000

Sales to a Joint Venture

When a contractor controls a joint venture and then sells materials and services to it, these transactions cannot be considered sales. Instead, they are treated as intercompany transactions. Once the joint venture completes the sale of those materials and services to a client that is *not* controlled by the contractor, the contractor can then recognize the sales.

Summary

The typical contractor will enter into a joint venture either on a 50:50 basis with one other party, or on a lesser ownership basis with several other parties. This means that a consolidation of the financial statements of the contractor with a joint venture entity is not likely. The most likely alternative is the equity method, since it applies whenever there are a few partners participating in a joint venture.

From the perspective of the accountant, the equity method can safely be described as time-consuming, since it requires significantly more tracking work than the vastly simpler accounting for an investment at its cost (which can be used if there is no significant influence over the investee). Consequently, if there is any question about the existence of significant influence, it is best to present an argument that does not favor use of the equity method.

Chapter 13
Construction Tax Issues

Introduction

The Internal Revenue Service (IRS) has a number of tax reporting requirements that are specific to the construction industry. The bulk of these requirements are stated on the IRS web site.[1] In this chapter, we address the essential tax issues pertaining to a construction business.

The Accounting Method to Use for Tax Reporting

A construction company must report its revenues and expenses on an income tax return in accordance with a method of accounting. An accounting method involves a set of rules, consistently applied, that show how and when to report revenue and expenses. As explained in a prior chapter, there are two general classifications of accounting methods, which are the cash method and the accrual method. Within the accrual classification are two alternative approaches, which are the percentage of completion method and the completed contract method. These alternatives appear in the following exhibit.

Alternative Accounting Methods

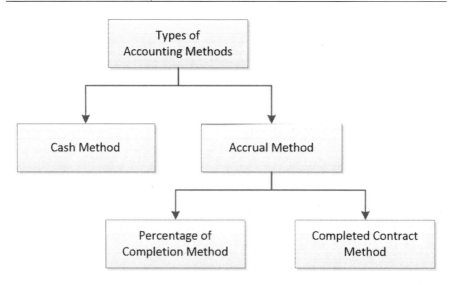

[1] *Accounting for Construction Contracts – Construction Tax Tips*, updated on August 23, 2016

From a taxation perspective, the method chosen should reasonably represent the income of the company. The method chosen is the correct one when:

- It consistently treats income and expenses in the same manner over time; and
- It is appropriate for the organization's line of work.

A construction business can use more than one accounting method when keeping its books for tax reporting purposes. One method is applied to all long-term contracts, while a separate method is used for all other contracts. A long-term contract is defined by the IRS as any contract that is not completed in the same year in which it was started.

EXAMPLE

Long Bow Construction uses the calendar tax year. The company begins a project on December 15 of 20X1 and completes it on January 15 of 20X2. According to the IRS rule for the classification of contracts, the project is classified as a long-term contract, even though its actual duration is only one month.

Long Bow begins another project on January 1 of 20X2 and completes it on December 31 of the same year. Since the project is completed entirely within one year, it is not classified as a long-term contract.

Application of the Cash Method

The cash method allows a company to recognize income when cash is received and expenses when cash is paid. The cash method can be used for all projects, even those classified as long-term.

The IRS imposes a condition on the standard rules for the cash method that were just noted. If the company pays an expense that benefits the company for more than one tax year, that expense must be spread over the period during which the benefit is received (which is essentially the accrual method of accounting).

EXAMPLE

Long Bow Construction pays $20,000 up front for a two-year lease on its office rent. The benefit to Long Bow is over two years, so the company must recognize $10,000 in each of the two years as an expense for tax purposes.

When a construction company is using the cash method, it may be tempting to defer taxable income by not depositing a check until a later accounting period. This is not allowed by the IRS, which uses the concept of *constructive receipt* to require that a check received in an accounting period is assumed to have been recorded on the books in that period. The key concept is that constructive receipt is assumed if the company could have received the money in one period but elected to not receive it until a later period.

EXAMPLE

At the end of December, the controller of Eskimo Construction receives in the mail a $25,000 check from a client. He puts the check in a desk drawer for a few days and then deposits it in January of the next year. Under the constructive receipt rule, the cash is assumed to have been received in December.

Also at the end of December, the ethically-challenged controller of Eskimo receives a call from another client located a few streets away, who says that he has cut a check to Eskimo for $5,000. The controller asks the client to hold the check and then walks over in early January to pick up the check. The same rule applies – the cash is assumed to have been received in December.

There are strict limitations on the use of the cash method, which are that it cannot be used when:

- The entity is a corporation or a partnership with a "C" corporation as a partner, whose average annual gross receipts are greater than $5 million.
- Total purchases of merchandise during the year are substantial when compared to the company's gross income. A further explanation of these terms follows.
  - *Merchandise* in the construction industry is more commonly re-ferred to as materials. For example, the concrete used in a building foundation is classified as merchandise for tax purposes.'
  - The IRS considers merchandise to be *substantial* when it is in the range of 10% - 15% of the company's gross income.

Application of the Accrual Method

If the limitations on the use of the cash method apply to a construction company, then the accrual method must be used. As noted previously, there are several variations on the accrual method that may be used. To determine which variation is most applicable, work through the following steps:

1. Classify all construction contracts as short-term or long-term. The overall method used by the company (either the cash basis or the accrual basis) is applied to all short-term contracts.
2. Classify all long-term contracts as home construction or general construc-tion. A home construction contract involves buildings with four or fewer dwelling units, where 80% or more of the estimated costs are for the con-struction, improvement, or rehabilitation of these units. All other contracts are classified as general construction.

EXAMPLE

Sunrise Construction is working on a duplex and an apartment building. The duplex has two dwelling units and so is classified as a home construction contract. The apartment building has more than four dwelling units and so is classified as a general construction contract.

3. If a contract is a long-term general construction contract, measure the average annual gross receipts of the business for the last three tax years. If the average is more than $10 million, the company is classified as a large contractor, and must account for these contracts using the percentage of completion method. When using this method, the business reports contract income each year according to the percentage of each contract that was completed in that year.

EXAMPLE

High Country Construction has completed 40% of an office building. The total estimated profit for the building is $1,000,000, so High Country must report $400,000 (that is, 40%) of the total profit in the current tax year.

4. If the average annual gross receipts of the business for the last three tax years are $10 million or less, the company is classified as a small contractor. In this case, the IRS requires that the company split its long-term general construction contracts into two categories. The first category is for those contracts that will likely be completed within two years of the start date. If a contract is expected to have more than a two-year duration, the large contractor method must be used.

EXAMPLE

Dozer Construction has had annual gross receipts for the last three tax years of $8.5 million. In the most recent year, Dozer had 15 contracts. Dozer's management estimates that 13 of the contracts will be completed within two years of their start dates, while the remaining two contracts will require a longer period to complete. Dozer should use the small contractor rules for the first 13 contracts and the large contractor rules for the two long-duration contracts.

EXAMPLE

Sleepy Hollow Construction had had annual gross receipts for the last three tax years of $12.4 million. Since the average gross receipts exceed $10 million, Sleepy Hollow must use the large contractor rules to account for all of its contracts. The rule for the estimated completion time that applied to small contractors does not apply.

> **Note:** The preceding analysis should be conducted annually, since the business may change over time, resulting in a different method of accounting.

As noted in the preceding Step 4, a small contractor must follow the large contractor method for longer-duration contracts. The large contractor method is the percentage of completion method. For shorter-duration contracts, the company is allowed to use any of the following methods to account for the contracts:
- Accrual method
- Percentage of completion method (PCM)
- Exempt percentage of completion method (ECPM)
- Completed contract method (CCM)

The accounting method variations for large and small contractors are noted in the following table.

Long-Term Contract Accounting Methods

Contractor Size	Accrual	PCM	ECPM	CCM
Large	No	Yes	No	No
Small	Yes	Yes	Yes	Yes

We will return to the different types of accrual methods shortly. First, we will address the types of costs that may be included in a construction contract.

Types of Costs

For tax purposes, there are two main types of costs that may apply to a construction project. These costs are:
- *Job costs.* These are expenses that are directly or indirectly associated with a project. Examples of these costs are materials, wages, subcontractor fees, equipment costs, and allocated indirect costs. Indirect costs include all expenditures needed to perform a contract other than direct costs. Examples of indirect costs are:
  - Administrative costs
  - Depreciation expense
  - Equipment insurance
  - Equipment rental
  - Indirect labor and contract supervisory wages
  - Indirect materials and supplies
  - Interest expense
  - Quality control
  - Repair and maintenance expenses for equipment and facilities
  - Taxes relating to labor, materials, supplies, equipment and facilities
  - Tools and equipment

o Utilities
- *General and administrative costs.* These are expenses associated with the ongoing operation of the business, and which cannot be traced back to specific jobs. Examples of these costs are rent, utilities, and office supplies. However, some of these costs can be allocated to projects as allocated indirect costs. For example, the compensation paid to a cost accountant who tracks project costs could be allocated to the projects on which he works.

Indirect job costs frequently benefit more than one job, and so these costs must be allocated among them.

EXAMPLE

Harkness Construction employs a buyer who acquires materials for three of the company's projects. The buyer's $50,000 compensation cost is allocated to the three projects based on the time that he spent on each one, as calculated in the following table.

Project	Hours Charged	Percentage	Allocation
A	1,000	50%	$25,000
B	700	35%	17,500
C	300	15%	7,500
Totals	2,000	100%	$50,000

Non-allocable job costs are charged to expense in the period in which they are incurred. These costs include the following:
- Advertising expenses
- Expenses for unsuccessful bids and proposals
- Marketing expenses
- Selling expenses

Types of Accrual Methods

This section provides an explanation of the different types of accrual methods that can be used for tax purposes. As noted in an earlier section, large contractors can only use the accrual method; the other methods are reserved for the use of small contractors.

Accrual Method

The IRS states that revenue can be recognized under the accrual method when all events have occurred that fix the company's right to receive payment and the amount of the payment can be determined with reasonable accuracy. This means that revenue is recognized on the earlier of any of these three events:
- When the revenue is earned (when completed to the customer's satisfaction)

162

- When the revenue is due (when the client is billed)
- When payment is received from the client

When a client makes an advance payment, the IRS advises that this payment be included in income when the payment is received. However, if the related service will not be performed until a subsequent year, it is allowable to delay the inclusion of this payment in income until that time.

For tax purposes, both job costs and general and administrative expenses are recognized in the tax year in which they are incurred. An expense is considered to have been incurred on the later of the following two dates:

- When the merchandise or services have been received; or
- When the amount of the expense can be accurately determined.

An outcome of this rule for expense recognition is that an expense can be deducted on a tax return before it is actually paid. As noted earlier, if the company pays for an expense that benefits it in more than one tax year, the expense must be equitably recognized over the periods during which the benefit is received.

Under the accrual method, the outlay for the purchase of a fixed asset is not immediately used as a deduction. Instead, the only deduction on a tax return is for the related amount of depreciation.

EXAMPLE

Calderon Construction enters into an agreement to build a garage for Mike Hodgson. Calderon uses the accrual method. The job takes one month to complete and is finished on December 20 of 20X1. Two days later, Calderon sends Hodgson a bill for $25,000, for which payment is received on January 8 of 20X2.

On December 5, 20X1, Calderon receives a $7,000 invoice from a nearby home supply store for the materials used in the construction of the garage. The bill is paid on January 3, 20X2. In addition, Calderon incurred general and administrative expenses of $3,000 in December.

Calderon recognizes the $25,000 revenue from the contract in 20X1, since the amount had been earned when the garage was completed in December. Further, the $7,000 of job costs and $3,000 of general and administrative costs are recognized in December, since that is when they were incurred.

The IRS allows a company to exclude retainages from the recognition of income until there is an unconditional right to receive them. If this election is made, the IRS also requires one to delay the recognition of any retainages payable until they have been paid.

Percentage of Completion Method

When a business has a contract that extends past the year end, it can make sense to use the percentage of completion method, since doing so will shift some of the taxable income associated with the project into the next year.

When using this method, indirect job costs should be allocated to long-term contracts for tax purposes. By doing so, some expenses are shifted into a future period, which increases the amount of reported taxable income in the current period. Since the tax liability is accelerated, this requirement favors the IRS.

Exempt Percentage of Completion Method

This method is only used for the calculation of taxable income; it is not used in the preparation of a company's financial statements. Under this approach, income from a long-term contract is recognized as the work progresses. This means that some income is reported in each year of the contract. To calculate the gross receipts from a contract for the current year, the calculation is:

1. Multiply the percentage complete by the total contract price
2. Subtract the amount of gross receipts previously reported for the contract

There are two valid approaches for computing income under this method, which are as follows:

- *Cost comparison method.* Divide the deductible job costs for the year by the estimated total job costs. Then multiply the resulting percentage by the contract price to arrive at the amount of income to report in the current tax year. All retainage receivable, pending change orders, and cost reimbursements must be included in the contract price.
- *Work comparison method.* Compute the completion factor by comparing the work performed thus far to the estimated amount of work to be completed. This calculation must be supported by appropriate documentation, or else by an architect or engineer. Expenditures are charged to expense as incurred.

EXAMPLE

Acorn Construction builds a greenhouse for Arborists International. Acorn estimates that the project will take four months, spanning the period October 1 to January 31 of the next year. The total contract price is $100,000, while the estimated total costs are $80,000. By the end of December, Acorn has billed the client $80,000 and spent $60,000 on job costs. Acorn's general and administrative expenses through this period are $5,000. Acorn's accountant computes taxable income as follows:

1. Percentage of completion is 75%, which is $60,000 costs incurred ÷ $80,000 estimated total job costs.
2. Multiply the 75% percentage of completion by the $100,000 contract price to arrive at $75,000 of income to report in the current year.
3. Subtract the $60,000 of job costs and $5,000 of general and administrative costs from the $75,000 of income to arrive at $10,000 of taxable profit.

EXAMPLE

Oak Construction is working on an office building, which is expected to last 12 months, beginning on April 1, 20X1 and finishing on March 31, 20X2. Oak uses the exempt percentage of completion method and the work comparison method.

The contract price is $1,000,000. By the end of 20X1, Oak has indeed completed 75% of the work (as certified by an engineer). Also by that date, Oak has incurred $700,000 of job costs and $20,000 of general and administrative expenses. Oak calculates its 20X1 taxable income as follows:

Contract price	$1,000,000
Percent complete	× 75%
20X1 taxable income	$750,000
Job costs	-700,000
General and administrative costs	-20,000
20X1 taxable net income	$30,000

The project is completed on schedule in March of 20X2. Oak finishes billing the customer and incurs an additional $130,000 of job costs and $5,000 of general and administrative costs. Oak calculates its 20X2 taxable income as follows:

Contract price	$1,000,000
Percent complete	× 100%
Total income	$1,000,000
Income reported in 20X1	-750,000
Income to be reported in 20X2	$250,000
Job costs	-130,000
General and administrative costs	-5,000
Year 2 taxable net income	$115,000

A key disadvantage of this method from the perspective of the taxpayer is that the recognition of income tends to be accelerated, so that an income tax liability arises sooner.

Completed Contract Method

Under the completed contract method, all revenue from contract and related job costs are recognized for tax purposes in the year when the project is completed.

When a business has a contract that extends past the year end, it can make sense to use the completed contract method for tax purposes, since doing so will shift all of the taxable income associated with the project into the next year. However, this means that the company's financial statements do not reflect the current status of projects. Also, income will tend to spike in those years when a disproportionate number of projects are completed. Further, losses on these contracts are not deductible for tax purposes until the projects have been completed. Given these issues, it is fairly common for companies to use the percentage of completion method for financial statement reporting purposes (to show better results), while using the completed contract method for tax reporting (to defer paying taxes).

When using this method, there may be a number of indirect costs charged to a job that are then capitalized, rather than being charged to expense as incurred. These capitalized costs are then deducted on the tax return when the project is completed. Doing so shifts some indirect expenses into a later period, which increases the amount of taxable income reported in the current period.

When this method is used, it is essential to separately track the costs of each job.

EXAMPLE

Atlas Construction is hired to build a factory for $900,000, with a start date of August 15, 20X1 and an estimated completion date of February 10, 20X2. Payment of the entire amount occurs upon client acceptance of the project. The estimated total costs for the project are $750,000. In early February, the work is finished and the client accepts the factory as complete.

At the end of 20X1, Atlas had $675,000 of costs associated with the contract. From that point until client acceptance, Atlas incurred another $75,000 of costs that were assigned to the project.

At the end of 20X1, Atlas has capitalized the $675,000 of costs incurred to date, so that they are stated as an asset on Atlas' balance sheet and have not been charged to expense. In February of 20X2, Atlas charges all $675,000 of the capitalized costs to expense, as well as the $75,000 of costs incurred in 20X2, for a total expense of $750,000. The entire $900,000 income from the project is also recognized in February of 20X2, so that Atlas reports $150,000 of taxable income in 20X2.

Summary

The different rules required by the IRS for revenue and expense reporting can be confusing to follow. A reasonable approach for making the tax rules less murky is to consult with a qualified tax advisor regarding the long-term tax reporting approach that management wants to use – and then stick to that approach over time. By doing so, the business can settle into a standard recordation procedure for reporting on its projects that it can follow with little variation into the future.

Chapter 14
Construction Accounting Controls

Introduction

Controls are needed to ensure that assets are not lost or stolen and that processes are followed in a consistent manner. Without controls, a company is much more likely to operate in a disorganized manner and to accumulate substantial losses. The need for controls is especially acute in the construction industry, where work is conducted off-site where activities and assets are more difficult to control. In this chapter, we will focus on just those controls that are of most use to a construction business. These are by no means all of the controls that could be applied – a number of more generic controls will be needed in addition to the ones stated in this chapter.

Segregation of Duties

In general, tasks related to purchasing, receiving, supplier payments, and employee payments should be split among at least two people. By doing so, it is much more difficult for any one person to both authorize a purchase and receive the resulting asset. Here are several ways in which activities can be split apart:

- A payables clerk prepares checks payable to suppliers and the company owner signs the checks.
- A payroll clerk prepares checks to employees and the company owner signs the checks.
- A buyer can order materials, but someone else receives them at the receiving dock.

An essential element of the segregation concept is that someone must authorize every payment. We just noted that a senior company officer signs checks, which is a form of authorization. In addition, here are several other controls in the same area:

- *Purchase order authorization.* A great many of the costs incurred involve purchase orders. A construction company needs to issue purchase orders so that it can keep track of the committed costs for a project. Since so many expenditures originate with purchase orders, one should be careful about who is authorized to issue them. For a higher level of control, implement password access to the purchase order module in the accounting system, so that only an authorized person can issue purchase orders from the system.
- *Unapproved supplier invoices.* The primary control over expenditures is the purchase order, so there must be a control to deal with supplier and subcontractor invoices for which there is no authorizing purchase order. At a minimum, a project manager must approve these invoices. At a higher level of control, the default treatment of these invoices is to automatically reject

them (though there could be repercussions if the invoices turn out to be valid).

The segregation of duties concept can be taken too far. If every possible supplier invoice must be approved, it can seriously delay company operations. Consequently, it may be quite acceptable to pay for smaller invoices without approval. Though these smaller amounts will then be unprotected by controls, the amount of any losses would be quite small.

Asset Tracking

A construction company maintains materials and construction equipment at its construction sites, as well as a small amount of unallocated inventory. These assets may be stolen, so there are several controls to consider that will mitigate the risk of asset theft. For example:

- *Lock down storage.* Construct a fence around the inventory storage area and keep the gate locked when there is no one overseeing the inventory.
- *Log out inventory.* When inventory items are removed from the storage area, create a written record of the jobs on which they will be used and log this information into the job cost ledger.
- *Count the inventory.* Conduct periodic inventory counts and reconcile any differences between the amounts counted and the amounts stated in the company's inventory records.
- *Count surplus materials.* There may be surplus materials stored at a job site when the work is complete. Since this is a less controlled environment, there is an increased risk of pilferage. Consequently, a reasonable control is to count surplus materials and adopt procedures for verifying that these items are later placed in storage in the company's warehouse facility.
- *Assign identification tags.* Permanently affix identification tags to all construction equipment, so that these items can be easily identified.
- *Track major assets.* Maintain a log of where all major construction equipment is located and who is responsible for each one.
- *Install security cameras.* It is easier for someone to steal materials from a job site, so install security cameras in those areas. Also consider the use of security guards to maintain watch over the assets.
- *Compare purchases to usage.* Compare the amounts of materials purchased to the amounts assigned to jobs. When there is a difference, theft may be occurring.

Access to Data

If someone wants to steal assets from the company, they can do so and then alter the accounting records to erase all traces of the assets. This is a particular concern in construction companies, which routinely order large quantities of materials, which could be misdirected. The following controls can be used to keep employees and outsiders from altering company records:

- *Lock down access.* Require password access to all key files in the company's computer systems, including the accounting, purchasing and receiving systems. Further, require periodic password changes by all users. Doing so drastically restricts access to just those people who need to update database information. Other users may be allowed read-only access to data, such as managers.
- *Turn on the change log.* Better business systems all offer a change log, which tracks the changes that have been made to the company database, as well as the names of the users who made the changes. This information can be used to track down deliberate attempts to hide the theft of assets.

Controls for Estimates and Bids

The estimates made as part of the bidding process are the foundation for the profitability of a contractor. If estimates are made incorrectly, a contractor will soon find that it either wins many competitive bids because its prices are unrealistically low, or that it is losing bids that it would normally win because of excessively high prices. Here are several controls that can be used to improve the odds of issuing reasonable bids:

- *Conduct secondary reviews.* Have a second person conduct an analysis of each major bid, verifying that all cost categories were addressed, as well as all features of the project specifications and drawings.
- *Conduct price matching.* Have an experienced staff person match the price estimates for materials, labor and subcontractors in a bid to other pricing information, such as published price lists and the labor rates stated in union contracts.
- *Verify clerical accuracy.* Recompile all costs and markups used in the derivation of a bid to ensure that the total is accurate.
- *Compare to rival bids.* Once a bidding process is complete, the bids of rivals may be made available by the owner. If so, compare them to the company's own bid package to see if there were any errors or assumptions in the company's bid that could be corrected in the future.
- *Use cost checklist.* When first devising a bid for a fixed fee pricing arrangement, use a standard checklist of costs that should be included in the formulation of the bid. It is entirely too easy to forget a major cost, which in turn is difficult for a reviewer to spot, since it is absent from the bidding documentation. Thus, a cost checklist that is based on costs incurred in previous jobs is an excellent way to reduce the risk of underbidding.

Controls for Cost Plus Pricing Arrangements

Project controls are especially necessary when a company is billing to a client under a cost plus pricing arrangement. In this situation, there is a strong temptation to add unauthorized costs to a project in order to bill these costs through to the customer, along with a profit percentage. If these overbillings are discovered, clients will be extremely unhappy about the situation. The following controls can be used to mitigate this risk:

- *Establish cost definitions.* Work with the client to develop a definition of each type of cost that is to be allowed within a job. This should include the contents of all overhead cost pools. A cost pool is a grouping of individual overhead costs, which are then allocated. Having cost definitions makes it easier to determine whether a cost should be included in or excluded from a job.
- *Establish allocation methodologies.* There may be a temptation to increase the allocation of overhead to a specific job, so that the allocated cost can be billed to a client. However, doing so will likely result in an irate client. Consequently, document at the start of a job the allocation calculations that will be used. The internal audit staff can then verify that the established allocation is being used throughout a job.
- *Establish expense approval process.* Have a member of management above the level of the project manager approve larger expenses before they are incurred. Doing so reduces the risk of incurring inappropriate expenses.
- *Review appropriateness of expenses.* It is possible that excessive or improper costs will be charged to a job. These can be difficult to detect, especially when the amounts charged are relatively small. Nonetheless, there should be a routine internal audit examination of job costs that delves into the applicability of charged expenses. When non-compliant expenses are found in a job record, the audit team should not only document these issues, but also trace them back to the person who authorized the original recordation. This may lead to further investigations into other costs authorized by the individual, to see if there is a pattern of over-charging jobs.

Controls for Fixed Fee Pricing Arrangements

When a company engages in fixed fee pricing arrangements, there is pressure for project managers to report a profit by the end of a contract. If so, a manager might be tempted to offload expenses elsewhere, rather than charging them to a project that is in danger of having a minimal profit or even a loss. The following controls can be used to mitigate this risk:

- *Establish profit responsibility.* Cost control is extremely important in a fixed fee pricing arrangement, so be sure to assign profit responsibility to the project manager. This person has control over billings and costs, and so is in the best position to ensure that planned profit levels will be attained. Without clear responsibility, costs are much more likely to increase beyond planned levels.
- *Review percentage of completion.* When a fixed fee arrangement spans a number of months, the contractor may be able to recognize some portion of the total revenue prior to final project completion. The estimation of the

amount of revenue to recognize is subject to fraud, since the information used for this determination can be altered and is subject to interpretation. To mitigate this risk, periodically have a third party review the calculation of the percentage of completion. Better yet, develop a documented methodology for calculating the percentage of completion and review the ability of managers to follow this process.

- *Conduct milestone reviews.* It is entirely possible under a fixed fee arrangement that the construction company will incur more costs than it can recover from the pricing structure of the underlying contract. If so, the amount of costs already incurred that will not be recovered must be charged to expense at once. To aid in making this decision promptly, build into the project timeline a series of milestone reviews. These reviews should examine the costs incurred to date and the projected costs required to complete the project and make a determination of whether any costs should be written off.

- *Monitor scope changes.* One of the chief causes of losses in a fixed fee arrangement is when the client demands changes in the scope of the job and the project manager does not respond with a change order to raise the price. Instead, the cost of the project spirals upward with no attendant increase in billings to the client. The best control over scope changes is proper training of the project manager in regard to the nature of scope changes and how to press for a change order. An additional control is to conduct periodic audits of open projects to see if scope creep has occurred without an attendant approval by the client of a change order.

Subcontractor Controls

A large part of the total expenditures for a job may be routed through subcontractors. If so, there is a clear need to ensure that the amounts paid to these entities are accurate. The following controls can be of assistance:

- *Match billings to contract.* Compare all subcontractor invoices to the authorizing contract to ensure that the amounts billed are reasonable. When there are several invoices that apply to a contract, keep an ongoing tally of the amounts billed, so that the total amount paid does not exceed the contractually authorized amount.

- *Approve subcontractor invoices.* When a subcontractor is working on a job for an extended period of time, there will likely be a number of progress billings. These billings are based on an estimate of the amount of work completed to date, which is difficult to determine. For this reason, subcontractor invoices should be approved by the project manager, who has the best knowledge of the actual progress that a subcontractor has achieved. The manager may want to travel to the job site to inspect the subcontractor's work before authorizing payment of an invoice.

When an invoice is received from a subcontractor, the company may be able to withhold a portion of the invoice until the client approves the project. By doing so, subcontractors have a strong incentive to provide quality work. In addition, applying a retention to invoices delays outbound cash flows, which can have a significant positive effect on the finances of the company. Thus, it is of some importance to ensure that retentions are properly identified and accounted for, as noted in the following controls:

- *Identify retentions.* Maintain a checklist of actions to take after a contract with a subcontractor is signed. One of the action items is to include on the company's subcontractor retention list the name of the subcontractor, the applicable retention percentage and the activities to which it applies. The retention amounts may vary by activity (such as none for materials and 20% for labor).

- *Distribute subcontractor retention checklist.* Include on a periodic department list of recurring activities an action item to issue the most recent update of the subcontractor retention checklist to the accounts payable staff, including the retrieval of all old checklists. Doing so ensures that the department staff is withholding retentions based on the latest information.

- *Automatically detect retentions.* The accounts payable module of the accounting system can be configured to automatically deduct the correct retention percentage from invoices received from each subcontractor.

- *Set up a payment trigger.* When a payable is shifted into the accounts payable – retention account, there is no trigger in the accounting system to ensure that these payments are eventually made to subcontractors. There are several ways to create a triggering mechanism. One is to include in the month-end closing process for the accounting department a step to review the contents of the retention account and pay out any retentions that are now due for payment. Another option is to include the retention payment activity on a checklist that is consulted whenever the company receives a retention payment from a client (which then obligates the company to pay its subcontractors). These two notification options can be combined for a more robust control.

Materials Controls

The cost of materials may be the largest part of the costs incurred by a contractor. A number of controls should be imposed over the purchase and handling of materials, since even a small percentage loss in this area can add up to a significant loss. These controls are:

- *Review stopgap purchase orders.* The manager of a construction project may need to occasionally issue stopgap purchase orders, which are orders placed at the last minute to ensure that materials are available to keep work moving on a construction site. These purchase orders are needed to keep a job moving when a materials shortage would otherwise halt work. However, stopgap purchase orders are created on short notice, with less regard to obtaining the best price. Consequently, it is useful to analyze the circumstances that caused each stopgap purchase order to be placed, to see if the situation can be remedied in the future.

- *Use three-way matching.* When a supplier invoice is received, compare it to the authorizing purchase order and receiving documentation to see if the price charged is the same price authorized and that the quantity received matches the authorized amount. If the price or quantity is incorrect, send the invoice to the project manager for approval of the variance.

- *Close unfilled purchase orders.* A supplier may not deliver the full number of units authorized by a purchase order. If so, and there is no further need for the undelivered goods, notify the supplier that the order has been cancelled. Otherwise, the company will be forced to accept any additional deliveries under the purchase order and then store them in inventory.

- *Automatically warn of excessive expenditures.* The accounts payable module of the accounting system can be configured to issue a warning when the aggregate amount of invoiced expenses for a particular expense category exceeds the amount authorized in a purchase order or contract. Depending on the system, a supervisory override may be needed to process payment on the excessive amounts.

- *Audit job cost records.* The information in the job cost ledger must be accurate, so that management has a full understanding of the profits and losses generated by each job. To ensure the accuracy of these records, periodically audit the materials entries in the job cost ledger, matching selected entries to source materials such as supplier invoices.

Labor Controls

It can be quite difficult to maintain a proper degree of control over construction labor costs, especially since employee time sheets are usually only submitted at the end of each week, which means that corrective action can only be taken at weekly intervals. Here are several ways to keep from expending too much on labor costs:

- *Approve all timesheets.* The project manager or foreman should review and approve the timesheets submitted by work site employees. This review should include an examination of the cost codes being charged, to ensure that costs are charged correctly. An even better control is to review worker timesheets on a daily basis, so that problems can be detected sooner.

- *Assign responsibility for cost overages.* When there is a labor cost overrun, assign responsibility for it to the work site supervisor. This person is in the best position to spot and correct labor reporting issues.

- *Audit local payrolls.* It is possible that the payroll function for a larger project resides at the job site, with the project manager having the authority to approve payments and sign paychecks. Since these payments can involve a substantial expenditure, it may be worthwhile for the corporate audit staff to periodically visit job sites and review the timesheet documentation associated with selected payrolls to see if there have been any unusual transactions.

- *Audit job cost records.* The labor amounts charged to each job must be accurate, so that management can see the true profitability of each job. To ensure the accuracy of these records, periodically audit the labor entries in the job cost ledger, matching selected entries to timesheet records.

Equipment Controls

The equipment costs charged to a job can be substantial, so it is necessary to maintain a reasonable set of controls over them in order to manage their costs. These controls are:

- *Return equipment promptly.* Equipment is usually charged to a job based on the number of hours or days that it is kept on the job site. Consequently, the work site supervisor should keep track of the on-site equipment and return it as soon as it is no longer needed.
- *Review equipment cost allocation.* The hourly or daily rate at which equipment is charged to a job depends in part on the compilation of the standard hourly charge. This standard rate is based on an estimate of the costs that will be incurred during the year, as well as the number of hours that the equipment will be used; both of these estimates could be incorrect, so it can make sense to review the standard allocation rate at regular intervals (such as quarterly) and adjust the rate to bring it into alignment with actual costs and usage levels.
- *Audit job cost records.* The equipment-related costs charged to a job may be incorrect, so periodically audit selected job cost records relating to equipment charges, to see how the costs were calculated and assigned.
- *Control equipment transfers.* Have a system in place for recording the transfer of equipment between jobs. Otherwise, there is a risk that equipment time will be undercharged to one job and overcharged to another.
- *Audit equipment locations.* Periodically conduct an audit of all equipment owned, rented, or leased by the company to see if the actual locations match the company's records. If not, there is a problem with the equipment record keeping and cost assignment systems.

Job Closure Controls

Once a job is complete, it should be closed down as soon thereafter as possible. Otherwise, someone could incorrectly shift a cost from an active job to an inactive job, thereby making the active job look more profitable than is really the case. Since few people review the costs for inactive jobs, there is a reduced chance that the shifting of costs will ever be noticed. The following controls can be used to deal with the situation:

- *Include closure on checklist.* Create a checklist of activities to be completed once a job is done, which includes the closure of the job in the job cost ledger.

- *Verify open jobs.* As part of the month-end closing process, discuss all open jobs with the project management staff to see if any can be closed.
- *Review entry log.* As a periodic internal audit procedure, examine the computer log of entries made to the job cost ledger, to see if entries have been made into jobs that have been closed or are open but inactive.
- *Password-protect closed jobs.* Only allow a more senior accounting person to access closed jobs, thereby minimizing the risk of having unauthorized activity in closed accounts.
- *Conduct closing review.* Once a job has been completed, conduct a formal written review of the project that states the revenues billed and expenses incurred. The project manager should sign off on this document, which is then securely archived. The reason for this review is to establish a record of the amount of approved costs incurred. If the project accounting records later reveal a different cost total, this indicates that the records were subsequently manipulated.

Of the preceding controls, the most critical one is the closing review. The reviewer should look for problems with a job that can be brought to the attention of management. If a solution is found, it can be applied to all other open jobs, as well as to all future jobs. In addition, if a best practice is spotted in a closed job, be sure to apply it to all other jobs.

Tip: Do not use the closing review to place blame on individuals. When this is the case, employees are more likely to hide problems. Instead, focus on how any problems found can be resolved.

Percentage of Completion Controls

A potential risk when using the percentage of completion to calculate project revenues is that the person making the estimate will falsely deliver a percentage that is too high. The result is the recognition of an excessive amount of revenue. There are a few ways to mitigate the risk of a false percentage of completion, such as:

- *Use alternative measures.* Periodically compare the baseline method for calculating the percentage of completion to a set of alternative measurements. Explore the reasons for any differences between the compiled measures.
- *Periodically reevaluate calculations.* The cost to complete a project is one of the key underpinnings of the percentage of completion calculation. This cost may increase over time due to wage and price escalations, so reevaluate the total cost calculation at reasonable intervals to see if this occurred. A significant increase in the total cost can result in a lower percentage of completion estimate when the estimate is based on costs incurred.

- *Use outsiders.* Occasionally bring in a qualified outsider, such as an architect, to evaluate the status of a project and provide a percentage of completion.

Change Order Controls

Change orders can cause a large amount of conflict between a contractor and its client, because there are disagreements about what was authorized and how much should be billed. These disputes can result in unexpected losses for a contractor, so it makes sense to adopt several controls to mitigate the number and size of losses related to change orders. Here are several possibilities:

- *Use an approval committee.* Form a committee that is comprised of representatives from the contractor and the client, and have them mutually agree upon what the changes will be and the associated price that will be charged.
- *Maintain a change order log.* When the committee receives a change request, it should enter the request into a change order log, so that no forms are inadvertently lost. The log should also state when the committee dealt with each request and the outcome of that analysis. Once a change order is approved by the committee, enter it into a separate log that is used for billing purposes, to ensure that each change order is billed to the client when the related work is completed.
- *Use approvals.* Convert all change orders into documents and have them signed by authorized representatives of both parties. Then make sure that the client has a copy of each change order.
- *Verify cost levels.* The amount of revenue to be billed under a change order should always match or exceed the amount of costs to be incurred. Otherwise, the contractor will lose money. Have an analyst review the more material change orders to ensure that all change orders are priced to at least break even, if not generate a profit.

Billing Controls

The billing environment in the construction industry is unique, because invoices are not necessarily prepared for clients when there is a delivery. Instead, billings may be prepared at intervals that are specified by the terms of individual contracts. For example, one contract may allow for a billing after a certain number of cubic yards of concrete have been poured for a runway, while another contract allows a billing when the framing for an apartment building has been completed.

Given the wide variability of the timing and amounts of billings, this is an unusually difficult billing environment where there is a high likelihood of billing errors and billings that may be missed entirely. Here are several controls to help deal with the situation:

- *Summarize billing terms.* Whenever a contract is signed with a client, send a copy to the accounting department, where the billing terms are extracted and summarized in a master billing schedule. This schedule is then used as a reference for when and how to bill clients.

- *Verify billings.* Some client billings can be inordinately complex, which makes them more likely to be protested or rejected by customers. To minimize the risk of a client rejection, have a second person verify each billing before it is released. Verification should include comparing the billing to the contract terms and ensuring that the amount billed does not exceed the maximum funding allowed by the contract.
- *Track retentions.* Since retentions may not be paid for months (or longer), the accounting staff tends to forget about them. To minimize the risk of not being paid retentions in a timely manner, record all retention amounts on a department schedule that states the amounts due and approximately when they should be paid – and then put the schedule on the department calendar, so that it is inspected at regular intervals.

Budget Controls

A construction job will likely have a detailed budget associated with it that states the costs and work hours expected to be incurred. This budget will only be useful as a control if it is properly managed. Here are several ways to do so:

- *Assign costs promptly.* Costs should be charged to a job as soon as possible, preferably within a day of their being incurred. By doing so, any resulting reports will include the most accurate actual costs.
- *Report promptly.* Budget versus actual costs should be reported to job managers on a very frequent basis, so that they can take action to correct problems while there is still time to do so.
- *Adjust the budget.* Most jobs have a contingency reserve for unexpected cost overruns. When a cost overrun occurs, use an internal change order to move funds from the reserve to those cost classifications that need the extra funds. Also, when costs are clearly not going to be incurred, shift the related budgeted funds back to the contingency reserve with an internal change order. By taking these steps, the budget remains a relevant benchmark against actual costs incurred.
- *Review specific cost overruns.* When everyone knows there will be a cost overrun in a certain expense area of a job, it is possible that the project manager will record any number of additional expenditures within that expense area. By doing so, the project appears to have a blowup in only one area, while the rest of the job looks like it is well-managed. Consequently, an accountant or analyst should be especially careful to review large cost overruns to see if costs were moved among accounts.

Financing Controls

A contractor may engage in *front-end loading*, where relatively high bid prices are assigned to job tasks near the beginning of a project. The result is large early cash payments, which assist in the financing of a project. However, this also means that the cash flows towards the end of a project will be relatively low, which can cause cash flow problems for a contractor. Accordingly, a reasonable control is to construct and routinely update a cash forecast for each job, estimating the dates and amounts of cash inflows and outflows. A quality cash forecast can warn management when there may be an impending cash crunch that will require outside financing.

The use of a cash forecast may be required by lenders, who will want to know when their loans will be repaid. Thus, the use of this control may be mandated by outside parties.

General and Administrative Controls

In the preceding sections, we have described a number of controls that can be applied to certain aspects of a business that are unique to the construction industry. This still leaves open the question of how to control general and administrative (G&A) expenses. We have already noted the use of purchase orders to control larger expenditures, which should certainly be applied to the larger G&A expenditures. In addition, a useful control is to plot G&A expenses on a trend line for each cost type for the past 12 months and investigate any unusual variances from the long-term trend.

Besides trend line analysis, another control over G&A costs is to construct a budget for each cost type and then monitor actual results against the budget in each reporting period. This approach can backfire in cases where the budget was too optimistic, or where the business climate changes so much that the budget no longer reflects reality. Both issues can be corrected by revisiting the budget at reasonable intervals and adjusting it as necessary.

Construction Fraud

The controls noted in this chapter might appear excessive, especially when considering that these controls are only the ones specific to the construction industry. There are many generic controls that must also be installed. There is a good reason for these controls, given the substantial number of frauds that can be perpetrated within the industry. Fraud is especially prevalent here, because there are so many factors that tempt people to engage in it. For example:

- Some of the projects being bid upon are so high-value that there is a temptation to bribe whoever is selecting the winner on behalf of the client.
- Government approval may be needed for a construction site, which raises the prospect of bribing government officials in order to gain expedited approval. The bribe paid could be in something other than cash, such as construction work on the property of a government official.
- Government bidding standards frequently require that the lowest bid be accepted, which gives contractors an incentive to grossly overcharge on other aspects of a job, such as change orders.

- An aggressive bidding process can result in few profits for contractors, so they may be tempted to restrict the number of bidders by agreement amongst themselves, thereby driving up the prices being bid on projects.
- It can be difficult to produce financial statements that will allow a contractor to obtain the requisite bonding required by a client. This means there is pressure to produce the best possible income statement and balance sheet, even if doing so results in wild fabrications.
- Some employees are day laborers who may only work on job sites for a short time and then move on to other work, so there is a temptation to not pay them for all hours worked or for overtime.
- When a project is designated as a cost reimbursement contract, the contractor is tempted to throw all possible costs at it. For example, construction equipment could be charged to a single job, rather than spreading this cost over many jobs. Or, administrative costs are reclassified as job costs and charged straight to jobs.
- When the percentage of completion method is being used, there is an incentive to under-represent the total cost of a job. By doing so, a project appears to be more complete than is actually the case, allowing the contractor to recognize a larger interim profit. This type of fraud is especially likely, given how hard it is to disprove the estimates associated with the calculation.
- When a loss is expected on a job, it is supposed to be recognized at once. The prospect of an imminent loss can lead project personnel to shift costs among jobs in order to manufacture a profit, thereby avoiding the loss.
- As costs pile up on a project, it is possible that the estimated profit will gradually decline over time. This is called *profit fade*; when there is a substantial amount of profit fade, and especially across several projects, it indicates that the project managers are not able to control costs. To avoid this situation, there is a temptation to shift costs away from those projects experiencing profit fade and into newer projects. This tends to be an ongoing fraud, as costs are continually juggled among projects in order to manufacture profits.
- It is difficult to maintain tight control over the building materials and construction equipment left at construction sites. This can lead to employees or outsiders pilfering these items.
- Given the variety of tasks and the number of workers on job sites, it is relatively easy for employees to deliberately waste time on jobs, resulting in significant labor cost overruns.
- The massive size of some jobs allows managers and others to insert personal costs into the job cost ledger and have them paid by clients with a low risk of being caught. For example, building supplies can be shunted to personal projects; since they are legitimately classified as building materials, there is no clear indication that they do not relate to a job.

Summary

A key problem with controls is deciding when to add more controls and when to stop. When there are too many controls, company processes can be severely slowed down by the need for cross-checks, verifications, and hand-offs. One way to deal with the situation is to only add a control when a loss occurs, so that the control is used to mitigate the loss if it were to occur again. Clearly, this approach always results in at least one loss. An alternative approach that is more proactive is to go over the system of controls at least once a year and modify the system based on the entity's risk profile – which will change over time. A variation is to reconsider the system of controls whenever there is a significant change in company processes, which results in a more rapid adjustment of controls.

Chapter 15
Job Analysis

Introduction

This chapter contains several analyses that can be used to discern how individual jobs are performing. The analysis of projected costs and variances is useful for projecting the eventual outcome of a job. Adjusting for the timing of billings results in a better current estimate of the profitability of a job. Finally, earned value management analysis can be used to determine the ongoing progress and cost situation of a project. These concepts are explained further in the following sections.

Projected Cost and Variance Analysis

The costs that will be incurred on a job can vary from expectations by a substantial amount, potentially resulting in a significant loss. To keep this from happening, the accountant should maintain a close watch over not only those costs incurred to date, but also those costs to which the company is committed over the remainder of each job. Committed costs are those costs which the firm has an obligation to pay. These costs are usually associated with a purchase order for goods or services that has already been issued, or a contract with a subcontractor to provide services. These costs are frequently for fixed amounts, so the accountant is well aware of the exact costs that will be incurred on future dates.

Committed costs are included in the more advanced accounting systems, which allow for these costs to be ported over to the accounting system from the purchasing and contract management systems. From there, the information is combined with the costs stored in the job cost ledger to arrive at an estimate of the final cost of a job. However, this information still lacks any future costs that will be incurred by the construction company itself, so the accountant will need to consult with the project manager in regard to these additional costs.

When a company only has a computerized accounting system with manual purchasing and contract systems, it will be necessary to combine these varying types of information into an electronic spreadsheet in order to arrive at the same information that could have been provided (in large part) by a more advanced system.

We will assume that the typical accountant does not have access to a comprehensive system and so uses an electronic spreadsheet to conduct the analysis. The analysis begins with the original cost estimate and adds subsequent change orders to arrive at the total estimated cost for the job. This information is derived at the level of each cost code, in order to provide a detailed view of the original cost estimates. This part of the analysis forms the basis of comparison for subsequent performance. The second part of the analysis compiles all costs to which the company has been committed, adds on all other costs that have already been billed to the company, and then adds on the estimated cost of completion. The resulting total cost of completion is compared to the original estimated cost to arrive at a favorable or unfavorable variance. A sample spreadsheet that contains this layout appears in the following exhibit.

Projected Cost and Variance Spreadsheet

A	B	C	D	E	F	G	H	I	J
				(C+D)				(F+G+H)	(E-I)
							Estimated	Total	
		Original	Change	Total	Committed	Billed	Additional	Latest	
Code	Description	Estimate	Orders	Estimate	Costs	Costs	Costs	Projection	Variance
1210	Lot clearing	$6,700	$500	$7,200	$6,700	$500	--	$7,200	--
1220	Fill dirt	4,200	--	4,200	4,500	--	--	4,500	-$300
1230	Rough grading	3,500	--	3,500	--	--	3,600	3,600	-100
1300	Demolition	7,200	--	7,200	4,000	2,500	500	7,000	200
1460	Gas service	3,900	1,500	5,400	3,900	=	1,000	4,900	500
		$25,500	$2,000	$27,500	$19,100	$3,000	$5,100	$27,200	$300

In the preceding exhibit, the original estimate plus change orders totaled $27,500, while the latest actual project costs totaled $27,200, resulting in a $300 favorable variance.

Because the cost breakdown in the spreadsheet is at the level of individual cost codes, the reader of this report has quite a clear idea of where cost problems are located.

Adjusting for the Timing of Billings

When actual billed revenues are compared to the expenses incurred to date in a project, the result may not be valid. Billings may be issued either early or late, or are in amounts that have no relationship to the amount of expenses incurred. For example:

- A company compiles all costs incurred during a month and issues an invoice to the client for these amounts, plus a profit, in the next month. This means that the timing of billings always results in low profitability on every job, until it is closed and the final billing reveals the true state of affairs.
- A company is operating in a tight construction market and so is able to charge a higher proportion of the total billing up front, with a reduced billing towards the end of the project. In this case, the project manager might believe that the project is initially profitable when it is actually incurring a loss.
- A client forces the company to only bill through its costs, so that profits are only billed at the end of the project. In this case, billings are proportionally lower than normal until the final billing.

In all of these situations, the interim profitability results for a project must be adjusted for any overbillings or underbillings. The easiest way to do so is to separately compile project information in a spreadsheet that shows how well a job is (or is not) performing against the plan.

A sample spreadsheet appears in the following exhibit that shows how the relationship between billings and costs and profits can be discerned. The exhibit contains the following processing steps:

1. Subtract the estimated amount of total costs from the total contract revenue to arrive at the estimated profit.

2. Divide the proportion of costs incurred to date by the total estimated cost and multiply the resulting percentage by the estimated profit to determine the proportion of the profit that had been earned.

3. Combine the amount of costs incurred to date and the earned profit, and compare the result to the total amount billed. This will result in either costs and profits being greater than billings or billings being greater than costs and profits. These outcomes appear in Columns I and J of the following exhibit.

Billing Status Spreadsheet

A	B	C	D	E	F	G	H	I	J
			(B – C)	Actual	(D×(E÷C))	(E + F) Costs &		(G – H) Costs &	(H – G) Billings
	Contract	Est. Total	Est.	to-Date	Earned	Earned	Total	Profits	> Costs
Job	Total	Cost	Profit	Costs	Profit	Profit	Billed	> Billings	& Profits
529	$100,000	$92,340	$7,660	$83,106	$6,894	$90,000	$96,500	$--	$6,500
530	275,000	269,100	5,900	215,280	4,720	220,000	214,000	6,000	--
531	192,000	180,700	11,300	124,683	7,797	132,480	125,000	7,480	--
532	605,000	562,300	42,700	213,674	16,226	229,900	232,000	--	2,100
	$1,172,000	$1,104,440	$67,560	$636,743	$35,637	$672,380	$667,500	$13,480	$8,600

The billing status spreadsheet is useful in situations where there is a clear overbilling or underbilling, since either scenario results in financial statements that misrepresent the true financial status of a job. For example, Job 529 in the exhibit has $6,500 in billings in excess of costs and profits. This means that the interim profits reported by the business are too high by $6,500. Only by including this adjustment factor into the analysis can the accountant determine the true status of the job. Conversely, Job 530 is underbilled by $6,000, so the interim profits being reported for it are $6,000 too low.

A potential problem with this spreadsheet is the qualitative nature of the numbers inserted into the estimated total cost column (which is Column C in the exhibit). If the estimating staff is not diligent in updating this estimated cost based on the latest conditions, it is entirely possible that the spreadsheet will generate estimated profit numbers that are incorrect, which then throws off the earned profit calculation. Consequently, it is critical to update the spreadsheet with a high degree of diligence.

Earned Value Management

Earned value management is an approach for determining the real status of a job, which is not always easy when looking at the time elapsed or the amount of funds expended. For example, if 25% of the funds allocated to a job have been expended, does that imply that the job is also 25% complete? In many cases in which a job has been incorrectly estimated, the expenditure of funds or the passage of time does not reflect the actual status of the job at all – usually, the project is well behind schedule, but there is no way to determine *how far* behind.

Earned value is a way to combine scope, schedule, and resource measurements, using the outcome to assess the performance and progress of a job. It uses an integrated baseline, against which performance is measured at various times over the term of a job. The following three dimensions are used:

- *Planned value.* This is the authorized budget that has been assigned to scheduled work, and does not include any management reserves.
- *Earned value.* This is the budget associated with the authorized work that has been completed. This amount cannot be greater than the planned value. This figure is frequently used to determine a job's percentage of completion.
- *Actual cost.* This is the realized cost incurred for the work performed on an activity during a specific period of time. There is no upper limit on this amount.

EXAMPLE

The management team of Latham Lumber has started a construction project to build a storage shed for the company's completed lumber products. The project is expected to take six days, where the first day is used to build a concrete pad, each subsequent day is used to build an additional wall, and the sixth day is used to build the roof. For simplicity, the project manager assumes that $25,000 will be expended on each of the six days, for a total project budget of $150,000. After the first day, $25,000 has been expended and the concrete pad has been completed, so the project is exactly on time and on budget.

On the second day, there were issues with the framing that called for an additional expenditure of $2,000; the work was not quite completed.

On the third day, the construction crew completed the first wall but only half of the second wall; the crew then went home early. The crew only spent $15,000 on the third day. At this point, the project manager wants to measure the earned value of the project. She calculates the following items:

- The planned value is $75,000, which is the total budget through three days.
- The earned value is $62,500, which is calculated as the entire budgeted amount for the first and second days, plus half of the amount for the third day (since half of the second wall was completed).
- The actual cost is $67,000, which is comprised of $25,000 of actual costs incurred on the first day, $27,000 on the second day, and $15,000 on the third day.

This information can be used to identify trends early on, so that one can address and correct problems right away, before they become large enough to have a negative impact on the outcome of an entire project.

The concept of earned value can be employed to calculate performance against the project schedule and performance against the project budget. These concepts are addressed in the following sub-sections.

Schedule Performance Index

The schedule performance index (SPI) compares the earned value of a job to its planned value. The calculation is:

$$SPI = Earned\ value \div Planned\ value$$

If the resulting SPI is less than one, the job being measured is potentially behind schedule. Conversely, if the SPI is greater than one, it may be running ahead of schedule. In the rare case where the SPI equals one, the job is running precisely on schedule.

EXAMPLE

To continue with the Latham Lumber example, the earned value through three days is $62,500, along with a planned value of $75,000. The schedule performance index is calculated as:

$$\$62,500\ Earned\ value \div \$75,000\ Planned\ value$$

$$= 83.3\%\ Schedule\ performance\ index$$

The SPI indicates that the project may be behind schedule. It appears to be progressing at 83% of the rate that was originally planned.

A low SPI is especially important near the end of a job, since there is little time remaining in which to take corrective action.

Cost Performance Index

The cost performance index (CPI) compares the earned value of a job to its actual cost. The calculation is:

$$CPI = Earned\ value \div Actual\ cost$$

This measurement is used to examine the cost efficiency of budgeted resources. If the CPI is less than one, there has been a cost overrun on the work completed to date. If the CPI is greater than one, costs are running less than expected on the work to date. When the cumulative CPI for the job to date is less than one, the job will need to run less than expected through its completion in order to come in at budget. If this does not appear to be feasible, consider increasing the budget.

EXAMPLE

To continue with the Latham Lumber example, the earned value through three days is $62,500, along with actual costs of $67,000. The cost performance index is calculated as:

$$\$62,500 \text{ Earned value} \div \$67,000 \text{ Actual cost}$$

$$= 93.3\% \text{ Cost performance index}$$

The CPI indicates that the project may be running over budget. If this 93.3% rate continues, the project will end up incurring $160,772, which is calculated as:

$$\$150,000 \text{ Total budget} \div .933 = \$160,772$$

Summary

The three techniques presented in this chapter can all be used to examine different aspects of a current job's performance. The required calculations are not difficult, but it can take some time to assemble the necessary information. Consequently, the accountant or analyst may be tempted to produce these analyses only at longer intervals. If so, the information may be too delayed to be of much use to management. Instead, consider setting up these analyses in standardized formats and running them approximately once a week.

Chapter 16
Business Structures

Introduction

When a construction business is founded, there is a significant risk that the owners will not only lose their entire investments, but also be personally liable for the ongoing debts of the organization. This situation arises when the owners do not give sufficient attention to the legal structure of the entity. However, the legal structures that can protect owners may also give them less control over the business and could present income tax challenges. In this chapter, we outline the advantages and disadvantages of the various forms of legal entity that can be used for an organization.

Sole Proprietorship

A sole proprietorship is a business that is directly owned by a single individual. It is not incorporated, so that the sole owner is entitled to the entire net worth of the business, and is personally liable for its debts. The individual and the business are considered to be the same entity for tax purposes. The advantages of a sole proprietorship are:

- *Simple to organize.* The initial organization of the business is quite simple. At most, the owner might reserve a business name with the secretary of state. It is also quite easy to upgrade to other forms of organization.
- *Simple tax filings.* The owner does not have to file a separate income tax return for the business. Instead, the results of the business are listed on a separate schedule of the individual income tax return (Form 1040).
- *No double taxation.* There is no double taxation, as can be the case in a corporation, where earnings are taxed at the corporate level and then distributed to owners via dividends, where they are taxed again. Instead, earnings flow straight to the owner.
- *Complete control.* There is only one owner, who has absolute control over the direction of the business and how its resources are allocated.

The disadvantages of a sole proprietorship are as follows:

- *Unlimited liability.* The chief disadvantage is that the owner is entirely liable for any losses incurred by the business, with no limitation. For example, the owner may invest $1,000 in a real estate venture, which then incurs net obligations of $100,000. The owner is personally liable for the entire $100,000. An adequate amount of liability insurance and risk management practices can mitigate this concern.

- *Self-employment taxes.* The owner is liable for a 15.3% self-employment tax (social security and Medicare) on all earnings generated by the business that are not exempt from these taxes. There is a cap on the social security portion of this tax ($118,500 in 2016). There is no cap on the Medicare rate – instead, the rate *increases* by 0.9% at certain threshold levels.
- *No outside equity.* The only provider of equity to the business is the sole owner. Funding usually comes from personal savings and debt for which the owner is liable. For a large increase in capital, the owner would likely need to use a different organizational structure that would admit multiple owners.

In brief, the unlimited liability imposed by a sole proprietorship is usually considered to completely outweigh all other aspects of this form of ownership. Its ability to avoid double taxation can be matched by an S corporation (as described in a later section), but the S corporation also keeps the owner from being personally liable for the obligations of the business.

Partnership

A partnership is a form of business organization in which owners have unlimited personal liability for the actions of the business, though this problem can be mitigated through the use of a limited liability partnership. The owners of a partnership have invested their own funds and time in the organization and share proportionally in any profits earned by it. There may also be limited partners in the business, who contribute funds but do not take part in day-to-day operations. A limited partner is only liable for the amount of funds he or she invested in the entity; once those funds are paid out, the limited partner has no additional liability in relation to the activities of the partnership. If there are limited partners, there must also be a designated general partner that is an active manager of the business; this individual has essentially the same liabilities as a sole proprietor.

A partnership does not pay income taxes. Instead, the partners report their share of the partnership's profit on their personal income tax returns. Because partners must pay income taxes on their shares of partnership income, they typically require some distribution of cash from the partnership in order to pay their taxes. If a partner elects to instead leave some portion of his or her share of a distribution in the partnership, this is considered an incremental increase in the capital contribution of that person to the business.

In those instances where a partnership recognizes a loss during its fiscal year, the share of the loss recognized by each partner in his or her personal tax return is limited to the amount of the loss that offsets each partner's basis in the partnership. If the amount of the loss is greater than this basis, the excess amount must be carried forward into a future period, where it can hopefully be offset against the future profits of the partnership. In essence, tax law does not allow a partner to recognize more on his or her tax return than the amount contributed into a partnership.

The key advantages of a partnership are as follows:

- *Source of capital*. With many partners, a business has a much richer source of capital than would be the case for a sole proprietorship.
- *Specialization*. If there is more than one general partner, it is possible for multiple people with diverse skill sets to run a business, which can enhance its overall performance.
- *No double taxation*. There is no double taxation, as can be the case in a corporation. Instead, earnings flow straight to the owners.

The disadvantages of a partnership are as follows:
- *Unlimited liability*. The general partners have unlimited personal liability for the obligations of the partnership, as was the case with a sole proprietorship. This is a joint and several liability, which means that creditors can pursue a single general partner for the obligations of the entire business.
- *Self-employment taxes*. A partner's share of the ordinary income reported on a Schedule K-1 is subject to the self-employment tax noted earlier for a sole proprietorship.

The risk associated with a partnership arrangement works well for limited partners, since their losses are limited to their own investments in the business.

Corporation

A corporation is a legal entity, organized under state laws, whose investors purchase shares of stock as evidence of their ownership in it. A corporation can potentially exist indefinitely. It also acts as a legal shield for its owners, so that they are generally not liable for the corporation's actions. A corporation pays all types of taxes, including income taxes, payroll taxes, sales and use taxes, and property taxes.

A private company has a small group of investors who are unable to sell their shares to the general public. A public company has registered its shares for sale with the Securities and Exchange Commission (SEC) and may also have listed its shares on an exchange, where they can be traded by the general public. The requirements of the SEC and the stock exchanges are rigorous, so comparatively few corporations are publicly-held.

The advantages of the corporation are as follows:
- *Limited liability*. The shareholders of a corporation are only liable up to the amount of their investments. The corporate entity shields them from any further liability.
- *Source of capital*. A publicly-held corporation in particular can raise substantial amounts by selling shares or issuing bonds.
- *Ownership transfers*. It is not especially difficult for a shareholder to sell shares in a corporation, though this is more difficult when the entity is privately-held.

The disadvantages of a corporation are as follows:
- *Double taxation*. Depending on the type of corporation, it may pay taxes on its income, after which shareholders pay taxes on any dividends received, so income can be taxed twice.
- *Excessive tax filings*. Depending on the type of corporation, the various types of income and other taxes that must be paid can add up to a substantial amount of paperwork.

There are two main types of corporation, which are the C corporation and S corporation.

C Corporation

The default form of corporation is the C corporation. It is taxed as a separate entity, for which the tax filing can be voluminous. Distributions to shareholders are made at the discretion of the board of directors of the company, in the form of dividends. A dividend is considered taxable income to the recipient (though it is not subject to self-employment taxes). This means that there *is* double taxation, where the corporation pays an income tax on its earnings and shareholders also pay a tax on dividends received. Despite the double taxation disadvantage, the C corporation structure is heavily used, because it can be owned by an unlimited number of shareholders. This gives it an unrivaled ability to attract capital from investors.

S Corporation

A variation on the standard corporation model is the S corporation. An S corporation passes its income through to its owners, so that the entity itself does not pay income taxes. The owners report the income on their tax returns, thereby avoiding the double taxation that arises in a regular C corporation. Some additional points regarding the S corporation are:
- There can be no more than 75 shareholders, so this approach is most suitable for smaller entities.
- All of the shareholders must agree to adopt the S corporation structure.
- Every shareholder must be a United States resident or citizen.
- A C corporation or a partnership cannot be a shareholder, though estates and certain trusts and charities can be investors.
- There can only be a single class of stock, which prevents preferential payments and voting privileges.

Limited Liability Company

A limited liability company (LLC) combines the features of corporations and partnerships, which makes them an ideal entity for many businesses. Their advantages are:
- *Limited liability*. The liability of investors is limited to the amount of their investments in the LLC.

- *Income flow through.* An LLC can be structured so that the income earned by the business flows directly through to investors. This means that the investors pay income taxes, rather than the LLC.
- *Management.* An LLC can be run by professional managers, rather than a general partner.
- *Number of investors.* There is no limitation on the number of investors in an LLC, as opposed to the maximum cap on an S corporation.
- *Multiple classes of stock.* An LLC can issue multiple classes of stock, which can be useful when providing special privileges to certain investors.

The disadvantages of an LLC include:
- *Differing structures.* Each state has implemented different rules regarding how an LLC is structured and operated. This can cause confusion regarding the risks to which investors are subjected, how the entity can be managed, and its tax effects.
- *Filing fees.* There will be annual government fees charged to maintain an LLC entity, though the amount may not be excessive (depending on the state).

Summary

The corporate structure provides real risk mitigation benefits for owners, since it shields their personal assets from losses. Each variation on the concept has its own foibles, including differences in taxation, varying levels of control, and differing types of stock that can be sold. Consequently, we have noted the key attractions and problems with each, so that the reader can select the type of organization that most closely fits his or her circumstances.

Glossary

A

Accelerated depreciation. The depreciation of fixed assets at a very fast rate early in their useful lives.

Account. A separate, detailed record associated with a specific asset, liability, equity, revenue, expense, gain, or loss.

Accounting. The systematic recordation of the transactions of a business.

Accounting equation. The concept that assets in the balance sheet should equal liabilities plus equity.

Accounting method. A set of rules, consistently applied, that show how and when to report revenue and expenses.

Accounts payable. The aggregate amount of an entity's short-term obligations to pay suppliers for products and services which the entity purchased on credit.

Accounts receivable. Short-term amounts due from buyers to a seller who have purchased goods or services from the seller on credit.

Accrual. A journal entry that is used to recognize revenues and expenses that have been earned or consumed, respectively, but for which the related source documents have not yet been received or generated.

Accrual method accounting. A method of recording accounting transactions for revenue when earned and expenses when incurred.

Accrued expense. An expense that has been incurred, but for which there is not yet any expenditure documentation.

Accumulated depreciation. The to-date amount of depreciation charged against an asset.

Adjusting entry. A journal entry that is used at the end of an accounting period to adjust the balance in a general ledger account.

Amortization schedule. A table that states the periodic payments to be made as part of a loan agreement.

Assets. Items of economic value that are expected to yield benefits to the owning entity in future periods.

B

Bad debt. An invoice for which payment is not expected.

Back charges. Billings for work performed by or paid for by one party which should have been handled by a different party.

Backlog. The additional amount of revenue expected to be earned from incomplete contracts and contracts that have not yet begun.

Balance sheet. A financial statement that presents information about an entity's assets, liabilities, and shareholders' equity.

Base unit. An entity's definition of what constitutes a fixed asset.

Bid. A formal offer by a contractor to perform specified work for a certain price.

Book value. The original cost of an asset, minus any accumulated depreciation and impairment charges.

C

Capitalization limit. The amount paid for an asset, above which it is recorded as a fixed asset.

Carrying amount. The cost at which an asset or liability is recorded on the books.

Cash method accounting. A method of recording accounting transactions for revenue when cash is received and expenses when cash is paid.

Change order. An addition to a contract, usually for the provision of additional work in exchange for an increase in the contract price.

Chart of accounts. A list of all accounts used by an entity.

Claim. An amount in excess of a contract that a contractor seeks to collect from a client, usually because of problems caused by the client.

Committed cost. A cost that has not yet been paid, but for which an agreement has been made that the cost will be incurred.

Completed contract method. A revenue recognition method used to recognize all of the revenue and profit associated with a project only after the project has been completed.

Consolidation. The practice of combining the financial statements of a parent entity and other entities in which it has a majority interest.

Constructive receipt. When cash is assumed to have been received if a business could have received the money in one period but elected to not receive it until a later period.

Contingency. A future event that cannot be predicted with certainty.

Contra account. An account that offsets the balance in another account with which it is paired.

Contractor. An entity that enters into an arrangement to build facilities or render services as delineated by a buyer.

Control account. A summary-level account in the general ledger. It contains aggregated totals for transactions that are individually stored in subsidiary-level ledger accounts.

Corporation. A legal entity where ownership is evidenced by the shares held by investors. A corporation acts as a legal shield for its owners.

Cost method. The practice of recording an investment at its cost on the books of the investor.

Cost plus contract. A contract that allows the contractor to be reimbursed for its costs, plus a cost markup.

Cost pool. A grouping of individual overhead costs, which are then allocated.

Credit. An accounting entry that either increases a liability or equity account, or decreases an asset or expense account.

Credit memo. A transaction used to reduce an account payable.

Current asset. An asset that is cash, or which will be converted into cash within one year.

Current liability. A liability that will be settled within one year.

D

Debit. An accounting entry that either increases an asset or expense account, or decreases a liability or equity account.

Debit memo. An internal accounting transaction used to offset a stray payables credit balance in an account.

Debt. An obligation payable to a lender, with interest.

Depreciation. The systematic reduction in the recorded cost of a fixed asset.

Derecognition. The removal of an asset or liability from the records of an organization.

Direct cost. A cost that is only incurred if a job exists.

Disposal account. An account that is used to record the gain or loss on the disposition of an asset.

Double entry accounting. A method of recording transactions that requires the recordation of at least one debit and credit for each transaction.

E

Early payment discount. A discount offered by a supplier when its customers pay early.

Employee. A person who provides services to an employer in accordance with the legal definition of an employee.

Glossary

Equipment ledger. A subsidiary ledger in which is stored the costs charged to individual equipment items.

Equity. The net amount of funds invested in a business by its owners, plus any retained earnings.

Equity method. The practice of recording the investor's share in the profits or losses of an investee; used when the investor has significant influence over the investee.

Expense. The reduction in value of an asset as it is used to create revenue.

Experience rating. The history of unemployment claims made by the employees of a business.

F

Financial statements. A collection of reports about an organization's financial results, financial position, and cash flows.

Finance lease. When the lessee has purchased the underlying asset in a leasing arrangement.

Fixed assets. Assets that are expected to have utility over multiple reporting periods, and whose cost exceeds the minimum capitalization level of a business.

Fixed fee contract. A contract in which the contractor commits to fulfill the requirements of a contract for a fixed price.

Front-end loading. When relatively high bid prices are assigned to job tasks near the beginning of a project. The result is large early cash payments, which assist in the financing of a project.

G

General ledger. The master set of accounts that summarize all transactions occurring within an entity.

Generally Accepted Accounting Principles. A cluster of accounting standards and common industry usage that are applied to the recordation of transactions and preparation and presentation of financial statements.

Gross pay. The total compensation to be paid to an employee before taxes and other deductions are subtracted.

I

Income statement. A financial statement that contains the results of an organization's operations for a specific period of time, showing revenues and expenses and the resulting profit or loss.

Indirect cost. A cost that does not go into the actual construction of a project, but which is still needed to ensure that the project is completed on time and within budget.

Indirect method. A method of presentation for the statement of cash flows that begins with net income or loss, and then adds or subtracts non-cash revenue and expense items to derive cash flows.

Inventory. An asset that will be consumed or sold within one year, as part of the normal operating activities of a business.

Invoice. A document submitted to a customer, identifying a transaction for which the customer owes payment to the issuer.

J

Job cost ledger. A subsidiary ledger in which is stored the costs charged to individual jobs.

Joint venture. An enterprise that is owned by two or more other entities as a separate business; it is intended to be for the benefit of the investing group.

Journal entry. A formal accounting entry used to identify a business transaction.

L

Lender. An entity that lends money in exchange for the payment of interest.

Liability. A legally binding obligation payable to another entity.

Long-term contract. Any contract that is not completed in the same year in which it was started, as per IRS regulations.

Lookback period. The use of information from historical periods to make a decision.

M

Mid-month convention. The assumption that a fixed asset was purchased in mid-month for depreciation purposes, irrespective of when it was actually purchased.

N

Net income. The excess of revenues over expenses.

Net pay. The amount paid to employees after all payroll taxes and other deductions have been subtracted.

Non-current assets. Assets that will be consumed in more than one year.

Non-current liabilities. Liabilities that will be settled in more than one year.

O

Operating lease. A lease in which the lessee has obtained the use of an asset for a period of time.

Overtime. A premium wage paid that is calculated as $1\frac{1}{2}$ times the regular wage rate, multiplied by those hours classified as overtime.

P

Participating mortgage loan. A loan in which the lender can participate in the results of the operations of the real estate operation being mortgaged.

Partnership. A business that is not incorporated and where ownership is split among two or more entities.

Payables. The obligation to pay suppliers for goods and services that were acquired on credit.

Payroll. The compensation paid to hired employees, as well as the associated taxes.

Period cost. A cost that relates to a specific period of time, such as a monthly rent payment.

Pre-contract costs. Costs incurred prior to the signing of a contract with a client.

Prepaid expense. An expense that has been paid for, but for which the underlying asset will not be entirely consumed until a future period.

Principal. The amount of a debt that was originally borrowed and which remains unpaid.

Profit. The amount by which sales exceed expenses.

Project fade. The gradual decline in the estimated profit of a job.

Purchase order. A legal document authorizing the purchase of goods from a supplier.

R

Remittance advice. A document that provides the detail concerning a payment that has been made.

Retainage. An amount withheld from a payment to a supplier until a milestone date has passed or the client's approval.

Retained earnings. The profits that a business has earned to date, less any dividends or other distributions paid to investors.

Retention. An amount withheld from a progress billing, to be paid when a job is complete and the client is satisfied.

Revenue. An increase in assets or decrease in liabilities caused by the provision of goods or services to customers.

Revenue recognition. The process of determining the amount and timing of when revenue is recognized, based on the underlying earnings process.

Reversing entry. A journal entry that is the reverse of the original entry that was recorded in the preceding period.

S

Salvage value. The estimated amount for which a fixed asset can be sold at the end of its useful life.

Shift differential. The extra amount paid to someone working a late shift.

Sole proprietorship. A business that is not incorporated, so that a single individual is entitled to the entire net worth of the business, and is personally liable for its debts.

Statement of cash flows. A financial statement that identifies the different types of cash payments made by a business to third parties (cash outflows), as well as payments made to the business by third parties (cash inflows).

Stock. Ownership shares in a business.

Summary task. Something that describes a set of activities.

T

Temporary difference. The difference between the carrying amount of an asset or liability in the balance sheet and its tax base.

Three-way matching. The comparison of a supplier invoice and related purchase order and receiving document by the accountant prior to payment.

Transaction. A business event that has a monetary impact on the financial statements.

U

Unit-price contract. An arrangement in which the client pays a specific price for each unit of output.

Useful life. The time period over which an asset is expected to be productive.

V

Vendor master file. A file in which is stored information about the suppliers with which a business has ongoing transactions.

W

Work package. A group of activities for which work is estimated, scheduled, monitored, and controlled.

Working capital. Current assets minus current liabilities.

Index

80832135R00117

Made in the USA
Columbia, SC
11 November 2017